# 'Knit one
# STYLE ONE

# Knit one
# S·T·Y·L·E O·N·E

## A NEW
## KNITTING COLLECTION
## FROM LESLEY STANFIELD

Macdonald Orbis

A Macdonald Orbis Book

© Macdonald & Co (Publishers) Ltd 1986, 1987

First published in Great Britain by
Orbis Publishing Ltd., London 1986

This edition published in 1987 by
Macdonald & Co (Publishers) Ltd
London & Sydney

A member of BPCC plc

Printed in Italy by New Interlitho S.p.A. - Milan

ISBN: 0 356 15289 8

Macdonald & Co (Publishers) Ltd
Greater London House
Hampstead Road
London
NW1 7QX

# CONTENTS

# INTRODUCTION

This is a round-up of most of my favourite themes in hand knitting. It's a varied collection because fashion doesn't dictate a single look any more and knitting offers such scope to the designer. There are many changes of pace from small, close-fitting sweaters to big, baggy ones, complete outfits and dazzling one-offs. Classics are up-dated to look very new and untraditional.

One trend throughout is an emphasis on shoulders. Shaped and padded or deep and dropped, there's hardly a natural shoulder in the book. The importance of line is one of the features which distinguish today's designs from some of the cosy, amorphous knitting of the past. Another is the availability of interesting yarns. So many new yarns appear each season that the knitter has an almost bewildering choice between sophisticated fashion yarns and familiar basics. Both are featured here, with colour another important ingredient. From rich tones through the brights to gentler pastels and neutrals, colour strongly influences the mood of a design. Clothes and accessories are also important factors in the style mix and should be experimented with. It's intriguing to find that the same sweater can look just as exciting with a smart suit as with army fatigues.

This isn't a book for the complete beginner, although any reasonably competent knitter could tackle the majority of the designs and the instructions have been made as explicit as possible. Just as important as skill with the needles is the ability to assess what will suit you when it's eventually knitted. Choose your style!

*Lesley Stanfield*

SMOKY PASTELS

# SMOKY PASTELS

## *ROSE QUARTZ*

**W**ITHOUT CLINGING TIGHTLY, THIS LONG RIBBED SWEATER SKIMS EVERY CURVE. WELL-DEFINED SHOULDERS STREAMLINE THE SHAPE EVEN MORE. DESIGNED BY GAYE HAWKINS

### MATERIALS
10 (11, 11) × 50 g balls Phildar Kid Mohair
Pair each 3¼ mm (No 10) and 3¾ mm (No 9) knitting needles
3¼ mm (No 10) circular knitting needle, 60 cm long
Cable needle
Shoulder pads

### MEASUREMENTS
To fit bust 81-86 (91-97, 102-107) cm, 32-34 (36-38, 40-42) in
Actual measurement – 96 (102, 108) cm, 38 (40, 42½) in
Length – 75 cm
Sleeve length – 41 (42, 43) cm
Figures in round brackets are for larger sizes

### TENSION
26 sts and 30 rows to 10 cm measured over slightly stretched rib on 3¾ mm needles

### ABBREVIATIONS
alt – alternate; beg – beginning; cm – centimetres; cont – continue; c 8 b – sl next 4 sts on to cable needle and hold at back, k 1 tbl, p 2, k 1 tbl, then across sts on cable needle work k 1 tbl, p 2, k 1 tbl; c 8 f – as c 8 b but hold cable needle at front; dec – decrease; foll – following; in – inches; inc – increase; k –

knit; m 1 – make 1 st by picking up the strand between sts and k it through the back of the loop; p – purl; patt – pattern; rem – remain(ing); rep – repeat; sl – slip; st(s) – stitch(es); st-st – stocking stitch; tbl – through back of loop(s); tog – together
Work instructions in square brackets the number of times given

### BACK
With 3¼ mm needles, cast on 125 (133, 141) sts.
**1st rib row (right side)** K 1 tbl, *p 1, k 1 tbl; rep from * to end.
**2nd rib row** P 1, *k 1, p 1; rep from * to end.
Rep these 2 rows for 5 cm, ending with a 2nd rib row.
**Inc row** [K 1 tbl, p 1] 15 (17, 19) times, [k 1 tbl, m 1, p 1, m 1] 3 times, k 1 tbl, m 1, [p 1, k 1 tbl] 24 times, p 1, [k 1 tbl, m 1, p 1, m 1] 3 times, k 1 tbl, m 1, [p 1, k 1 tbl] 16 (18, 20) times.
139 (147, 155) sts.
Change to 3¾ mm needles.
Cont in patt thus:
**1st row and every foll alt row (wrong side)** Rib 31 (35, 39), [k 2, p 2] 3 times, k 2, [p 1, k 1] 24 times, p 1, [k 2, p 2] 3 times, k 2, rib 31 (35, 39).
**2nd row** Rib 31 (35, 39), [p 2, k 2 tbl] 3 times, p 2, [k 1 tbl, p 1] 24 times, k 1 tbl, [p 2, k 2 tbl] 3 times, p 2, rib 31 (35, 39).
**4th row** As 2nd.
**6th row** Rib 30 (34, 38), c 8 b, c 8 f, [p 1, k 1 tbl] 23 times, p 1, c 8 b, c 8 f, rib 30 (34, 38).
**8th row** As 2nd.
**10th row** As 2nd.
These 10 rows form patt.
Rep 1st to 10th rows twice, then work 1st to 9th rows again.
Keeping patt correct, shape sides thus:
**Dec row (right side)** Rib 4, k 3 tog, patt to last 7 sts, k 3 tog tbl, rib 4.
Patt 19 rows.
Rep last 20 rows once, then work dec row again. 127 (135, 143) sts.
Patt 63 (61, 59) rows straight, ending with a 3rd (1st, 9th) patt row. A total of

143 (141, 139) rows of patt have now been completed.

### Armhole Shaping
Keeping patt correct, cast off 4 sts at beg of next 4 rows. Dec 1 st at each end of next row and every foll alt row until 103 (111, 119) sts rem.
Patt 27 rows straight, ending with a 1st (9th, 7th) patt row. A total of 181 (179, 177) rows of patt have now been completed.
Inc 1 st at each end of next row and every foll 4th row until there are 117 (125, 133) sts.
Patt 3 (5, 7) rows, ending with a 9th patt row.

### Shoulder Shaping
Cast off 19 (21, 23) sts at beg of next 4 rows. Leave rem 41 sts on a spare needle.

### POCKET LININGS
**Make 2** With 3¾ mm needles, cast on 28 sts. Work 12 cm in st-st, ending with a p row.
Break off yarn and leave sts on a stitch holder.

### FRONT
With 3¼ mm needles, cast on 125 (133, 141) sts.
Rep 1st and 2nd rib rows of back for 5 cm, ending with a 1st rib row.
Change to 3¾ mm needles and rib a further 39 rows.
**Dec row (right side)** Rib 4, k 3 tog, rib to last 7 sts, k 3 tog tbl, rib 4. 121 (129, 137) sts. Rib 11 rows.
**Pocket Opening row (right side)** Rib 22 (26, 30) sts, sl next 28 sts on to a stitch holder, work across sts of 1st pocket lining, thus – [k 1 tbl, p 1] 3 times, [k 1 tbl, m 1, p 1, m 1] 3 times, k 1 tbl, m 1, [p 1, k 1 tbl] 7 times, p 1, rib next 21 sts of front, sl next 28 sts on to a stitch holder, work across sts of 2nd pocket lining thus – [p 1, k 1 tbl] 7 times, [m 1, p 1, m 1, k 1 tbl] 3 times, m 1, p 1, [k 1 tbl, p 1] 3 times, k 1 tbl, rib

22 (26, 30). 135 (143, 151) sts.
Beg with 3rd patt row of back (noting that there are 2 sts less at each end of rows), patt 7 rows.
Rep dec row as back.
Patt 19 rows.
Rep dec row. 127 (135, 143) sts.
Patt 47 (45, 43) rows straight, ending with a 7th (5th, 3rd) patt row.

### Neck Shaping
**1st row (right side)** Patt 63 (67, 71) sts, turn.

Cont on these sts only for 1st side and leave rem sts on a spare needle.
**\*\*** Dec 1 st at neck edge on next row and every foll 4th row until 59 (63, 67) sts rem.
Patt 2 rows, ending with a 3rd (1st, 9th) patt row. Thus front matches back to armholes.

### Armhole Shaping
Cont to dec at neck edge on every 4th row from previous dec, AND AT THE SAME TIME, cast off 4 sts at beg of next row and on the foll alt row. Patt 1 row – omit this row on 2nd side of neck.
Dec 1 st at armhole edge on next row and on the foll 3 alt rows.
Cont to dec at neck edge only until 37 (41, 45) sts rem, ending with a 1st (9th, 7th) patt row.
Still dec at neck edge as before, inc 1 st at armhole edge on next row and every foll 4th row until a total of 7 incs have been worked. 38 (42, 46) sts.
Patt 3 (5, 7) rows straight, thus front matches back to shoulder.

### Shoulder Shaping
Cast off 19 (21, 23) sts at beg of next row.
Patt 1 row. Cast off rem 19 (21, 23) sts.
**Next row** With right side facing, sl centre st on to a safety pin, rejoin yarn to inner end of rem 63 (67, 71) sts and patt to end.
Complete to match 1st side from **\*\*** but patt 1 extra row before starting armhole shaping and 1 extra row before starting shoulder shaping.

### SLEEVES
With 3¼ mm needles, cast on 53 (57, 61) sts.
Rep 1st and 2nd rib rows of back for 5 cm, ending with a 2nd rib row.
Change to 3¾ mm needles.
Working inc sts into rib, cont in rib inc 1 st at each end of 3rd row and every foll 4th row until there are 85 (91, 97) sts, then on every foll 3rd row until there are 105 (111, 117) sts.
Rib straight until sleeve measures 41 (42, 43) cm from cast-on edge, ending with a wrong-side row.

### Top Shaping
Cast off 4 sts at beg of next 4 rows.
Dec 1 st at each end of next row and every foll alt row until 65 (71, 77) sts rem, then on every row until 39 (41, 43) sts rem.
**Cast off row** K 1, *k 2 tog, lift 1st st on right needle over 2nd st and off needle; rep from * to end. Break off yarn and secure last st.

### NECKBAND
Join both shoulder seams.
**1st round** With right side facing and using 3¼ mm circular needle, beg at left shoulder, pick up and k 68 (72, 76) sts evenly down left front neck, k st from safety pin and mark this st with a contrast thread, pick up and k 68 (72, 76) sts evenly up right front neck then k across 41 sts of back neck. 178 (186, 194) sts.
Cont in rounds thus:
**2nd round** [K 1, p 1] to within 2 sts of marked st, k 2 tog, k 1, k 2 tog tbl, p 1, [k 1, p 1] to end of round.
**3rd round** K 1 tbl, [p 1, k 1 tbl] to within 2 sts of marked st, k 2 tog tbl, k 1, k 2 tog, [k 1 tbl, p 1] to end of round.
Rep 2nd and 3rd rounds until neckband measures 3 cm from pick up round.
Cast off evenly in rib, dec at centre as before.

### POCKET TOPS
With right side facing and using 3¼ mm needles, rib 3 cm as set across sts of pocket.
Cast off in rib.

### MAKING UP
Join side and sleeve seams. Set in sleeves. Sew down pocket linings on wrong side and sides of pocket tops on right side. Sew in shoulder pads.

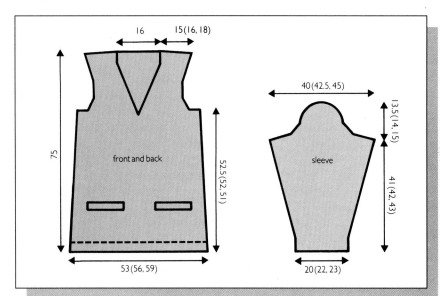

16    15 (16, 18)

front and back

75    52.5 (52, 51)

53 (56, 59)

40 (42.5, 45)

sleeve

13.5 (14, 15)

41 (42, 43)

20 (22, 23)

# AMETHYST

SHARP, SQUARE SHOULDERS AND AN UNUSUAL TWISTED CABLE ARE FEATURES OF THIS MODERN SKINNY RIB. A CLOSE-FITTING BALACLAVA SLIPPED INSIDE THE POLO NECK COMPLETES THE LOOK. DESIGNED BY PAT QUIROGA

## MATERIALS

**Sweater**
8 (9, 10) × 50 g balls Lister Motoravia 4 Ply

**Balaclava**
2 × 50 g balls Lister Motoravia 4 Ply
Pair 3 mm (No 11) knitting needles
Set of four 3 mm (No 11) double-pointed needles
Shoulder pads

## MEASUREMENTS

To fit bust 81-86 (91-97, 102-107) cm
32-34 (36-38, 40-42) in
Actual measurement – 90 (100, 111)
cm, 35½ (39, 43½) in
Length – 57 (58, 60) cm
Sleeve length – 45 cm
Figures in round brackets are for larger sizes

## TENSION

34 sts and 40 rows to 10 cm measured over patt on 3 mm needles

## ABBREVIATIONS

alt – alternate; beg – beginning; cm – centimetres; cont – continue; dec – decrease; foll – following; in – inches; inc – increase; k – knit; p - purl; patt – pattern; psso – pass slipped stitch over; rem – remain(ing); rep – repeat; sl – slip; st(s) – stitch(es); tog – together
Work instructions in square brackets the number of times given

## BACK

With pair of 3 mm needles, cast on 103 (115, 127) sts.

**1st row (right side)** P 1, *k 1, p 1; rep from * to end.
**2nd row** K 1, *p 1, k 1; rep from * to end.
Rep these 2 rows 15 times, then work 1st row again.
**Inc row** Inc in 1st st, *p 1, k into top of loop of st below next st on left needle then k into st on needle; rep from * to last 2 sts, p 1, inc in last st. 155 (173, 191) sts.
Cont in patt thus:
**1st row (right side)** *P 5, k 1, p 3; rep from * to last 2 sts, p 2.
**2nd row** K 2, *k 3, p 1, k 5; rep from * to end.
**3rd and 4th rows** As 1st and 2nd rows.
**5th row** *P 2, k 1, p 2, k 1, p 3; rep from * to last 2 sts, p 2.
**6th row** K 2, *k 3, p 1, k 2, p 1, k 2; rep from * to end.
**7th to 14th rows** Rep 5th and 6th rows 4 times.
**15th row** *P 2, sl next 7 sts on to a double-pointed needle, turn needle clockwise a half turn then work p 3, k 1, p 2, k 1 across these sts; rep from * to last 2 sts, p 2.
**16th row** K 2, *p 1, k 2, p 1, k 5; rep from * to end.
**17th row** *P 5, k 1, p 2, k 1; rep from * to last 2 sts, p 2.
**18th row** As 16th.
**19th to 24th rows** Rep 17th and 18th rows 3 times.
These 24 rows form patt.
Rep 24 rows 4 times.

### Armhole Shaping

Keeping patt correct, cast off 9 (11, 11) sts at beg of next 2 rows.
Dec 1 st at each end of next 7 (11, 11) rows, then on the foll 2 (5, 5) alt rows. 119 (119, 137) sts **.
Patt 59 (55, 61) rows straight.

### Shoulder Shaping

Cast off 10 (9, 12) sts at beg of next 2 rows, 10 (10, 13) sts on the foll 2 rows and 11 (10, 13) sts on the next 2 rows.
Leave rem 57 (61, 61) sts on a spare needle.

## FRONT

Work as back to **.
Patt 39 (35, 35) rows straight.

### Neck Shaping

**1st row** Patt 38 (36, 45) sts, turn.
Cont on these sts only for 1st side and leave rem sts on a spare needle.

Dec 1 st at neck edge on the next 7 rows. 31 (29, 38) sts.
Patt 12 (12, 18) rows straight.

### Shoulder Shaping

Cast off 10 (9, 12) sts at beg of next row and 10 (10, 13) sts on the foll alt row.
Patt 1 row. Cast off rem 11 (10, 13) sts.
**Next row** With right side facing, sl centre 43 (47, 47) sts on to a stitch holder, rejoin yarn to inner end of rem 38 (36, 45) sts and patt to end.
Complete to match 1st side working 1 row more before working shoulder shaping.

## SLEEVES

With pair of 3 mm needles, cast on 49 sts.
Work rib and inc row as for back. 74 sts.
Working inc sts into patt, cont in patt inc 1 st at each end of 7th row and every foll 6th (4th, 4th) row until there are 80 (114, 118) sts, then at each end of every foll 6th row until there are 110 (128, 128) sts.
Patt 35 (19, 23) rows straight, thus ending with a 24th patt row.

### Top Shaping

Cast off 9 (11, 11) sts at beg of next 2 rows. Dec 1 st at each end of next 7 (11, 11) rows. 78 (84, 84) sts. Dec 1 st at each end of every alt row until 74 sts rem.
Patt 49 (45, 51) rows straight, thus ending with a 14th (20th, 2nd) patt row.

### 1st size only

**Next row** P 2 tog, *[k 1, p 2 tog] twice, p 1, p 2 tog; rep from * 7 times.
**Next row** *K 3, p 1, k 1, p 1; rep from * 7 times, k 1.
**Next row** P 1, *sl 1, k 2 tog, psso, p 3 tog; rep from * 7 times.
**Next row** *K 1, p 1; rep from * to last st, k 1.
Cast off rem 17 sts.

### 2nd size only

**Next row** *P 2 tog, p 1, p 2 tog, k 1, p 2 tog, k 1; rep from * 7 times, p 2 tog.
**Next row** K 1, *p 1, k 1, p 1, k 3; rep from * 7 times.
**Next row** *P 3 tog, sl 1, k 2 tog, psso; rep from * 7 times, p 1.
**Next row** *K 1, p 1; rep from * to last st, k 1.

across these 79 sts. 119 sts. Working forwards and back in rows, cont in patt as back. Work the 24 patt rows twice, then work 1st to 16th rows again. Mark centre st with a coloured thread.

### Shape peak and crown
**1st row (right side)** Inc in 1st st, patt to within 2 sts of marked st, p 2 tog, k marked st, p 2 tog, patt to last st, inc in last st.
**2nd row** Patt as set.
Rep these 2 rows twice.
**Next row** As 1st row.
**Next row** Inc in 1st st, patt to within 2 sts of marked st, k 2 tog, p 1, k 2 tog, patt to last st, inc in last st.
Rep these 2 rows twice. Cast off.
Press lightly avoiding rib edging.
Fold cast-off edge in half and join seam.

### Edging
**1st round** With right side facing, rejoin yarn to the 1st of the 23 sts on stitch holder, rib across these 23 sts, pick up and k 58 sts evenly up 1st side to peak, pick up and k 1 st from peak and mark this st with a coloured thread, pick up and k 58 sts evenly down 2nd side then rib across 24 sts on stitch holder. 164 sts.
**2nd round** Rib to within 1 st of marked st, inc in next st, k 1, inc in next st, beg p 1 rib to end.
**3rd round** Rib to marked st, k 1, rib to end.
Rib 7 rounds, inc each side of marked st on 1st and every alt round.

Cast off rem 17 sts.
**3rd size only**
**Next row** *P 2 tog, p 1, p 2 tog, k 1, p 2 tog, p 1; rep from * 7 times, p 2 tog.
**Next row** K 3, *p 1, k 5; rep from * 6 times, p 1, k 3.
**Next row** P 3 tog, *sl 1, p 2 tog, psso, p 3 tog; rep from * 6 times, sl 1, p 2 tog, psso, p 1.
**Next row** *K 1, p 1; rep from * to last st, k 1.
Cast off rem 17 sts.

### COLLAR
Join both shoulder seams.
With right side facing, using set of 3 mm needles and beg at left shoulder seam, pick up and k 15 (15, 19) sts evenly down left front neck, k across 43 (47, 47) sts at centre front, pick up and k 15 (15, 19) sts up right front neck then k across 57 (61, 61) sts of back neck. 130 (138, 146) sts.
Divide sts evenly over 3 needles.
Work 14 cm in rounds of k 1, p 1 rib.
Cast off loosely in rib.

### MAKING UP
Press lightly, avoiding rib edgings.
Join side and sleeve seams. Set in sleeves. Sew in shoulder pads.

### BALACLAVA
Cast on 126 sts evenly over 3 double-pointed needles.
Work 11 cm in rounds of k 1, p 1 rib – on last round mark st 102 with a coloured thread.
Break off yarn. Sl first 23 sts and last 24 sts of round on to stitch holders.
With wrong side facing, rejoin yarn to marked st and work inc row as back

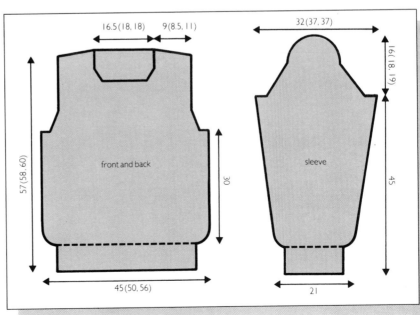

# FRENCH DRESSING

## BON CHIC

**B**OLD CHEVRONS
DRAMATIZE A
LUXURIOUS JACKET,
BLENDING SOFTLY
TEXTURED YARNS IN
MUTED SHADES OF
GREY. DESIGNED BY
LESLEY STANFIELD

### MATERIALS
8 (9) × 50 g balls Anny Blatt Mohair et
Soie shade Zinc (M)
3 (4) × 50 g balls Anny Blatt Bright
shade Acier (A)
2 (3) × 50 g balls Anny Blatt Bright
shade Gris (B)
1 × 50 g ball Anny Blatt Starblitz shade
Mars (C)
1 × 50 g ball Anny Blatt Laser shade
Blanc (D)
Pair each 5½ mm (No 5) and 6½ mm
(No 3) knitting needles
7 buttons
Shoulder pads

### MEASUREMENTS
To fit bust 86-91 (97-102) cm, 34-36
(38-40) in
Actual measurement – 112 (118) cm,
44 (46½) in
Length – 66 (67) cm
Sleeve length – 44 cm
Figures in brackets are for larger size

### TENSION
12 sts and 16 rows to 10 cm measured
over st-st on 6½ mm needles

### ABBREVIATIONS
alt – alternate; beg – beginning; cm –
centimetres; cont – continue; dec –
decrease; foll – following; in – inches;
inc – increase; k – knit; m-st – moss
stitch; p – purl; patt – pattern; rem –
remaining; rep – repeat; sl – slip; st(s) –
stitch(es); st-st – stocking stitch; tog –
together

### NOTE
Starblitz is used double throughout

### BACK
With 5½ mm needles and M, cast on
69 (73) sts.
**1st row (right side)** K 1, *p 1, k 1; rep
from * to end. (M-st).
Rep 1st row 7 times more.
Change to 6½ mm needles.
Beg k, work 14 rows st-st.
Mark last row with a contrast thread.
**\*\*** Cont in patt thus:
**1st row (right side)** K 34 (36) M, 1 D,
34 (36) M.
**2nd row** P 34 (36) M, k 1 D, p 34 (36)
M.
Do not strand yarn across the back of
work for any further colour changes.
Use a separate small ball of yarn for
each area of colour and twist yarns at
every colour change (see notes on
colour knitting on page 108).
**3rd row** K 33 (35) M, 1 D, 1 A, 1 D, 33
(35) M.
**4th row** P 33 (35) M, k 1 D, p 1 A, k 1
D, p 33 (35) M.
**5th row** K 32 (34) M, 1 D, 3 A, 1 D, 32
(34) M.
**6th row** P 32 (34) M, k 1 D, p 3 A, k 1
D, p 32 (34) M.
Cont to patt thus, working 1 st less
with M at each end of every right-side
row and 2 sts more with A in centre,
until 30 rows have been worked from
**\*\***.
**31st row** K 19 (21) M, 1 D, 14 A, 1 C,
14 A, 1 D, 19 (21) M.
**32nd row** P 19 (21) M, k 1 D, p 14 A,
k 1 C, p 14 A, k 1 D, p 19 (21) M.
**33rd row** K 18 (20) M, 1 D, 14 A, 1 C,
1 B, 1 C, 14 A, 1 D, 18 (20) M.
**34th row** P 18 (20) M, k 1 D, p 14 A,
k 1 C, p 1 B, k 1 C, p 14 A, k 1 D, p 18
(20) M.
**35th row** K 17 (19) M, 1 D, 14 A, 1 C,
3 B, 1 C, 14 A, 1 D, 17 (19) M.

BON CHIC

FRENCH DRESSING

**36th row** P 17 (19) M, k 1 D, p 14 A, k 1 C, p 3 B, k 1 C, p 14 A, k 1 D, p 17 (19) M.
Cont to patt thus, working 1 st less with M at each end of every right-side row and 2 sts more with B in centre, until 44 rows have been worked from **.

**Armhole Shaping**
Keeping patt correct, dec 1 st at each end of next and every row until 53 (55) sts rem.
Patt straight until 80 (82) rows have been worked from **.

**Neck Shaping**
**Next row** Patt 19 (20) sts, turn.
Keeping patt correct, cont on these sts only for 1st side.
Leave rem sts on a spare needle.
Dec 1 st at neck edge on next 3 rows.

**Shoulder Shaping**
Cast off 10 sts at beg of next row.
Work 1 row.
Cast off rem 6 (7) sts.
Leave centre 15 sts on a stitch holder.

**Next row** With right side facing, rejoin yarn to inner end of rem 19 (20) sts and patt to end.
Complete to match 1st side.

**POCKET LININGS**
**Make 2** With 6½ mm needles and M, cast on 16 sts.
Work in st-st for 16 rows.
Break off yarn and leave sts on stitch holder.

**LEFT FRONT**
With 5½ mm needles and M, cast on 32 (34) sts.
**1st row (right side)** *K 1, p 1; rep from * to end.
**2nd row** *P 1, k 1; rep from * to end. (M-st.).
Rep 1st and 2nd rows 3 times more.
Change to 6½ mm needles.
Beg k, work 16 rows st-st.**
**Pocket opening row** K 10 (12), sl next 16 sts on to a stitch holder, k across sts of one pocket lining, k 6.
Work 3 rows straight. Mark last row with a coloured thread.

*** Cont in patt thus:
**1st row** K 31 (33) M, 1 D.
**2nd row** K 1 D, p 31 (33) M.
**3rd row** K 30 (32) M, 1 D, 1 A.
**4th row** P 1 A, k 1 D, p 30 (32) M.
Cont in patt, working 1 st less with M and 1 st more with A on every right-side row until 30 rows have been worked from ***.
**31st row** K 16 (18) M, 1 D, 14 A, 1 C.
**32nd row** K 1 C, p 14 A, k 1 D, p 16 (18) M.
**33rd row** K 15 (17) M, 1 D, 14 A, 1 C, 1 B.
**34th row** P 1 B, k 1 C, p 14 A, k 1 D, p 15 (17) M.
**35th row** K 14 (16) M, 1 D, 14 A, 1 C, 2 B.
**36th row** P 2 B, k 1 C, p 14 A, k 1 D, p 14 (16) M.
**37th row** K 13 (15) M, 1 D, 14 A, 1 C, 3 B.
**38th row** P 3 B, k 1 C, p 14 A, k 1 D, p 13 (15) M.

**Armhole Shaping**
Cont patt, dec 1 st at beg of next row, then dec 1 st at this edge on every row until 24 (25) sts rem.
Patt straight until 62 (64) rows have been worked from ***.

**Neck Shaping**
**Next row** Patt 20 (21) sts, turn.
Keeping patt correct, cont on these sts only.
Leave rem sts on a stitch holder.
Dec 1 st at beg of next row, then dec 1 st at this edge on alt rows until 16 (17) sts rem.
Patt straight until front matches back to shoulder, ending at side edge.

**Shoulder Shaping**
Cast off 10 sts at beg of next row.
Work 1 row.
Cast off rem 6 (7) sts.

**RIGHT FRONT**
Work as left front to **.
**Pocket Opening row** K 6, sl next 16 sts on to a stitch holder, k across sts of one pocket lining, k 10 (12).
Work 3 rows straight. Mark last row with a coloured thread.
*** Cont in patt thus:
**1st row** K 1 D, 31 (33) M.
**2nd row** P 31 (33) M, k 1 D.
**3rd row** K 1 A, 1 D, 30 (32) M.
**4th row** P 30 (32) M, k 1 D, p 1 A.
Cont in patt until 30 rows have been

worked from ***.

**31st row** K 1 C, 14 A, 1 D, 16 (18) M.
**32nd row** P 16 (18) M, k 1 D, p 14 A, k 1 C.
**33rd row** K 1 B, 1 C, 14 A, 1 D, 15 (17) M.
**34th row** P 15 (17) M, k 1 D, p 14 A, k 1 C, p 1 B.
Cont in patt until 38 rows have been worked from ***.

## Armhole Shaping
Cont in patt, dec 1 st at end of next row, then dec 1 st at this edge on every row until 24 (25) sts rem.
Patt straight until 62 (64) rows have been worked from ***.

## Neck Shaping
**Next row** Patt 4 sts and sl these 4 sts on to a stitch holder, patt 20 (21).
Dec 1 st at end of next row, then dec 1 st at this edge on alt rows until 16 (17) sts rem.
Complete to match left front.

## SLEEVES
With 5½ mm needles and M, cast on 29 (33) sts.
Work 8 rows as beg of back.
Change to 6½ mm needles.
Beg with a k row, work 12 rows st-st (lengthening or shortening sleeves here if necessary).
Mark last row with a contrast thread.
* Inc 1 st at each end of next and every 4th row until 14 rows have been worked from *.
Cont in patt thus:
**1st row** K 18 (20) M, 1 D, 18 (20) M.
**2nd row** P 18 (20) M, k 1 D, p 18 (20) M.
**3rd row** Inc 1 st at each end of row, k 18 (20) M, 1 D, 1 A, 1 D, 18 (20) M.
**4th row** P 18 (20) M, k 1 D, p 1 A, k 1 D, p 18 (20) M.
Cont in patt, working 1 st less with M at each end of every right-side row and 2 sts more with A in centre, AT THE SAME TIME inc 1 st at each end of every 4th row until there are 49 (53) sts.
Patt 3 rows straight.
Inc 1 st at each end of next and every alt row until there are 61 (65) sts, ending with a wrong-side row.

## Top Shaping
Dec 1 st at each end of every row until 45 (49) sts rem.
Cast off loosely.

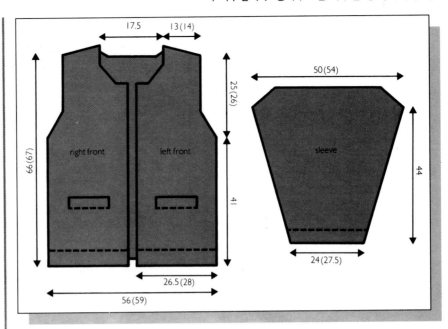

## POCKET TOPS
With right side facing, using 5½ mm needles and M, work 8 rows m-st as left front across sts on stitch holder.
Cast off in m-st.

## LEFT FRONT BAND
With 5½ mm needles and M, cast on 6 sts.
Work in m-st as left front until band fits front to neck shaping, ending with a right-side row.
Break yarn and leave sts on holder.
Starting 2 cm from lower edge, mark position of 6 buttons along band and allowing for 7th to occur on 4th and 5th rows of neckband.

## RIGHT FRONT BAND
As left, working 6 buttonholes to correspond with markers but ending with a wrong-side row.
Work buttonhole thus:
**1st row** M-st 2, cast off 2, m-st 2, including st already on needle.
**2nd row** M-st 2, cast on 2, m-st 2.
Leave sts on a stitch holder.
Do not break yarn.

## NECKBAND
Join shoulder seams.
With 5½ mm needles and M, with right side of work facing, m-st 5 sts of right front band, p tog last st of band and 1st st of right neck, k 3 rem sts from holder, pick up and k 18 (20) sts round side neck, k 15 sts from back neck, pick up and k 18 (20) sts round side neck, k 3 sts from neck holder, p

tog last st of left neck and 1st st of left front band, m-st rem sts of band. 69 (73) sts.
**2nd and 3rd rows** M-st as set.
**4th row** M-st 12, k 3 tog, m-st 7 (9), k 3 tog, m-st 19, k 3 tog, m-st 7 (9), k 3 tog, m-st 8, cast off 2, m-st to end.
**5th row** M-st 2, cast on 2, m-st to end.
Work 2 rows m-st.
Cast off in m-st.

## MAKING UP
Press lightly. Sew on front bands. Sew down pocket linings on wrong side and sides of pocket tops on right side. Set in sleeves. Sew side and sleeve seams. Sew on buttons. Sew in shoulder pads. The long 'snarls' of Laser can be teased out with a needle for an extra textured effect.

COUNTRY CALENDAR

# COUNTRY CALENDAR

## SYCAMORE

A CLOUD OF SOFT MOHAIR IS ETCHED WITH AUTUMN LEAVES AND EDGED WITH TWISTED RIB. DESIGNED BY LESLEY STANFIELD

### MATERIALS
9 × 50 g balls Jaeger Mohair Gold
Pair each 4 mm (No 8) and 5 mm (No 6) knitting needles

### MEASUREMENTS
One size, to fit up to bust 102 cm, 40 in
Actual measurement – 114 cm, 45 in
Length – 63 cm approx
Sleeve length – 43 cm

### TENSION
16 sts and 22 rows to 10 cm over rev st-st on 5 mm needles

### ABBREVIATIONS
alt – alternate; beg – beginning; cm – centimetres; cont – continue; dec – decrease; foll – following; in – inches; inc – increase; k – knit; p – purl; patt – pattern; psso – pass slipped stitch over; rem – remain(ing); rep – repeat; rev st-st – reverse stocking stitch; sl – slip; st(s) – stitch(es); t 2 – k into front of 2nd st on left-hand needle then k into front of 1st st slipping both sts off left-hand needle tog; tbl – through back of loop; tog – together; yfwd – yarn forward; yon – yarn over needle; yrn – yarn round needle

### NOTE
When working from charts read rows alternately from right to left (all right-side rows) then left to right (all wrong-side rows).

Take care not to work too tightly into sts that are worked tbl (through back of loop), as they should separate and 'ladder' when work is pressed

### BACK
With 4 mm needles, cast on 91 sts.
**1st rib row (right side)** P 1, * t 2, p 1; rep from * to end.
**2nd rib row** K 1, *p 2, k 1; rep from * to end.
Rep 1st and 2nd rib rows until work measures 8 cm, ending with a 2nd rib row and inc 1 st at each end of last row. 93 sts.
Change to 5 mm needles.
Beg p, work 10 rows in rev st-st.

#### Small leaf patt
**1st row (right side)** P 12, *work 13 sts of row 1 of Chart 1, p 1; rep from * twice, work 13 sts of row 1 of Chart 1, p 26.
**2nd row** K 26, *work 13 sts of row 2 of Chart 1, k 1; rep from * twice, work 13 sts of row 2 of Chart 1, k 12.
**3rd to 22nd rows** As 1st and 2nd rows but working rows 3 to 22 of chart.

#### Long leaf patt
**1st row (right side)** P 19, *work 13 sts of row 1 of Chart 2, p 1; rep from * 3 times, work 13 sts of row 1 of Chart 2, p 5.
**2nd row** K 5, *work 13 sts of row 2 of Chart 2, k 1; rep from * 3 times, work 13 sts of row 2 of Chart 2, k 19.
**3rd to 31st rows** As 1st and 2nd rows but working rows 3 to 31 of chart.
Beg k, work 3 rows in rev st-st.

#### Large leaf patt
**1st row (right side)** P 5, work 27 sts of row 1 of Chart 3, p 1, work 27 sts of row 1 of Chart 3, p 33.
**2nd row** K 33, work 27 sts of row 2 of Chart 3, k 1, work 27 sts of row 2 of Chart 3, k 5.
**3rd to 35th rows** As 1st and 2nd rows but working rows 3 to 35 of chart **.
Beg k, work 19 rows in rev st-st.

### Shoulder Shaping
P 83, turn, sl 1, k 72, turn, sl 1, p 62, turn, sl 1, k 52, turn, sl 1, p 41, turn, sl 1, k 30.
Sl all 93 sts on to a spare needle.

### FRONT
Work as back to **.
Beg k, work 5 rows in rev st-st.

### Neck Shaping
**Next row** P 37, turn. Cont on these sts only for 1st side and leave rem sts on a spare needle.
Dec 1 st at neck edge on the next 6 rows. 31 sts.
Work 4 rows straight, thus ending with a p row.

### Shoulder Shaping
K 21, turn, sl 1, p to end, k 11, turn, sl 1, p to end.

### Eyelet band
**1st row (wrong side)** P across all 31 sts of shoulder.
**2nd row** K 1, *yfwd, sl 1, k 1, psso; rep from * to end.
**3rd row** P.
Leave 31 sts on a spare needle.
With right side facing, sl centre 19 sts on to a stitch holder, rejoin yarn to inner end of rem 37 sts and complete to match 1st side.

### SLEEVES
With 4 mm needles, cast on 43 sts.
Rib 8 cm as at beg of back, but end with a 1st rib row and omit increases.
**Inc row** K twice into 1st st, *p 2, k 1, p 2, k twice into next st; rep from * to end. 51 sts.
Change to 5 mm needles.
Beg p, work 6 rows in rev st-st, inc 1 st at each end of 1st and 5th rows. 55 sts.

### Long leaf patt
**1st row (right side)** P 14, *work 13 sts of row 1 of Chart 2, p 1; rep from * once, work 13 sts of row 1 of Chart 2.
**2nd row** *Work 13 sts of row 2 of

COUNTRY CALENDAR

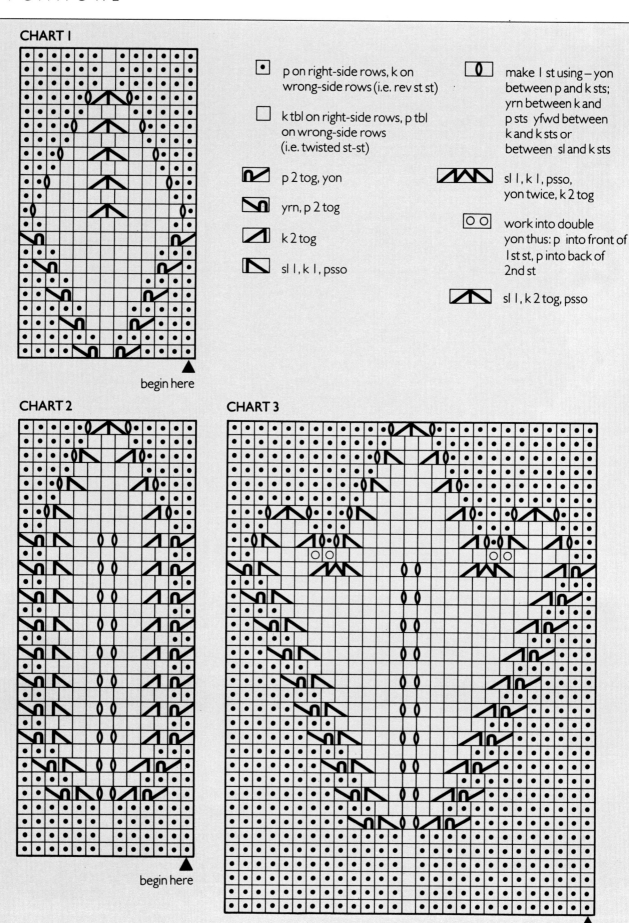

**CHART 1**

begin here

| | |
|---|---|
| • | p on right-side rows, k on wrong-side rows (i.e. rev st st) |
| ☐ | k tbl on right-side rows, p tbl on wrong-side rows (i.e. twisted st-st) |
| ⬓ | p 2 tog, yon |
| ⬓ | yrn, p 2 tog |
| ⬓ | k 2 tog |
| ⬓ | sl 1, k 1, psso |

| | |
|---|---|
| ◖ | make 1 st using – yon between p and k sts; yrn between k and p sts  yfwd between k and k sts or between  sl and k sts |
| ⩚ | sl 1, k 1, psso, yon twice, k 2 tog |
| ○ ○ | work into double yon thus: p into front of 1st st, p into back of 2nd st |
| △ | sl 1, k 2 tog, psso |

**CHART 2**

begin here

**CHART 3**

begin here

right sides tog, and needles parallel, with 5 mm needle k 1 st from each needle tog, AND AT THE SAME TIME, cast off 31 sts.

With right side facing and using 4 mm needles, pick up and k 16 sts down left front neck (including eyelet band), k 19 sts at centre front, pick up and k 16 sts up right front neck then k across first 31 sts of back neck. 82 sts.

Beg with 2nd rib row, rib 5 cm as at beg of back.

Cast off very loosely in rib.

## MAKING UP

Join left shoulder as right by casting off sts tog. Press carefully, opening out all leaf sts to form 'veins'. Join ends of neckband, then fold neckband in half on to wrong side and catch down. With centre of cast-off edge of sleeves to shoulder seams, sew on sleeves. Join side and sleeve seams. Press seams.

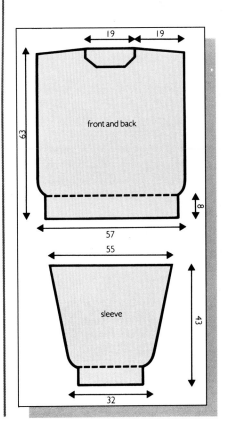

Chart 2, k 1; rep from * once, work 13 sts of row 2 of Chart 2, k 14.

**3rd to 31st rows** Inc 1 st at each end of next row and every foll 4th row, work as 1st and 2nd rows but working rows 3 to 31 of chart. (N.B. Work inc sts in rev st-st).

It may help to mark 1st st of 1st patt rep and last st of last rep with a contrast thread and carry this up the work every row so that the extra sts at each side can be counted easily.

Beg k, and inc as before, work 5 rows in rev st-st. 73 sts.

### Small leaf patt

**1st row (right side)** P 2, *work 13 sts of row 1 of Chart 1, p 1; rep from * twice, work 13 sts of row 1 of Chart 1, p 16.

**2nd row** K 16, *work 13 sts of row 2 of Chart 1, k 1; rep from * twice, work 13 sts of row 2 of Chart 1, k 2.

**3rd to 22nd rows** Inc as before, work as 1st and 2nd rows, but working rows 3 to 22 of chart.

Cont in rev st-st, inc as before, until there are 89 sts.

Cont straight until sleeve measures 42 cm from cast-on edge, ending with a p row.

### Eyelet band

Work 1st to 3rd rows as given for front shoulder, working over all 89 sts of sleeve.

Cast off loosely purl-wise.

### NECKBAND

Join right shoulder seam thus: with

COUNTRY CALENDAR

# SILVER BIRCH

CABLED IN HEAVY SILK, A TRACERY OF WINTER BRANCHES GLEAMS AND DRAPES SUPERBLY. DESIGNED BY MELODY GRIFFITHS

## MATERIALS
750 g (800 g, 900 g, 950 g) Maxwell Cartlidge Aran Silk
Pair each 4 mm (No 8) and 5 mm (No 6) knitting needles
Cable needle

## MEASUREMENTS
To fit bust 81 (86, 91, 97) cm, 32 (34, 36, 38) in
Actual measurement – 107 (111, 116, 120) cm, 42 (43½, 45½, 47) in
Length – 54 (54, 57, 57) cm
Sleeve length – 46 cm
Figures in brackets are for larger sizes

## TENSION
18 sts and 22 rows to 10 cm over st-st on 5 mm needles

## NOTE
In wear tension of garment may differ, thus measurements may vary slightly from those above

## ABBREVIATIONS
beg – beginning; cm – centimetres; cont – continue; dec – decrease; in – inches; k – knit; m 1 – make 1 st by picking up the strand between sts and on right-side rows p it through the back of the loop or on wrong-side rows k it through the back of the loop; p – purl; patt – pattern; rem – remaining; rep – repeat; rev st-st – reverse stocking stitch; sl – slip; st(s) – stitch(es); st-st – stocking stitch; tog – together

## BACK
With 4 mm needles, cast on 98 (102, 106, 110) sts.
**1st rib row (right side)** K 2, *p 2, k 2; rep from * to end.
**2nd rib row** P 2, *k 2, p 2; rep from * to end.
Rep 1st and 2nd rib rows 9 times.

Change to 5 mm needles.
**\*\*Next row** K 6, p 86 (90, 94, 98), k 6.
**Next row** P 6, k 86 (90, 94, 98), p 6 **\*\***.
Rep last 2 rows 2 (2, 4, 4) times.
Cont in patt thus:
**1st row (right side)** K 6, p 8 (10, 12, 14); reading row 1 of Chart 1 from right to left work over next 70 sts thus – p 11, k 4, p 10, k 6, p 8, k 6, p 10, k 4, p 11; p 8 (10, 12, 14), k 6.
**2nd row** P 6, k 8 (10, 12, 14); reading row 2 of Chart 1 from left to right work over next 70 sts thus – k 11, p 4, k 10, p 6, k 8, p 6, k 10, p 4, k 11; k 8 (10, 12, 14), p 6.

Cont in this way until all 80 rows of chart have been worked.
Work from **\*\*** to **\*\*** 1 (1, 2, 2) times.
Cont in st-st **\*\*\***.
Beg with a k row, work 10 rows.

## Neck Shaping
**1st row** K 37 (38, 39, 40), turn.
Cont on these sts only for 1st side.
Dec 1 st at neck edge on the next 4 rows. 33 (34, 35, 36) sts.
Work 2 rows straight. Leave sts on a spare needle.
**Next row** With right side facing, sl centre 24 (26, 28, 30) sts on to a stitch

**CHART 1**

**CHART 2**

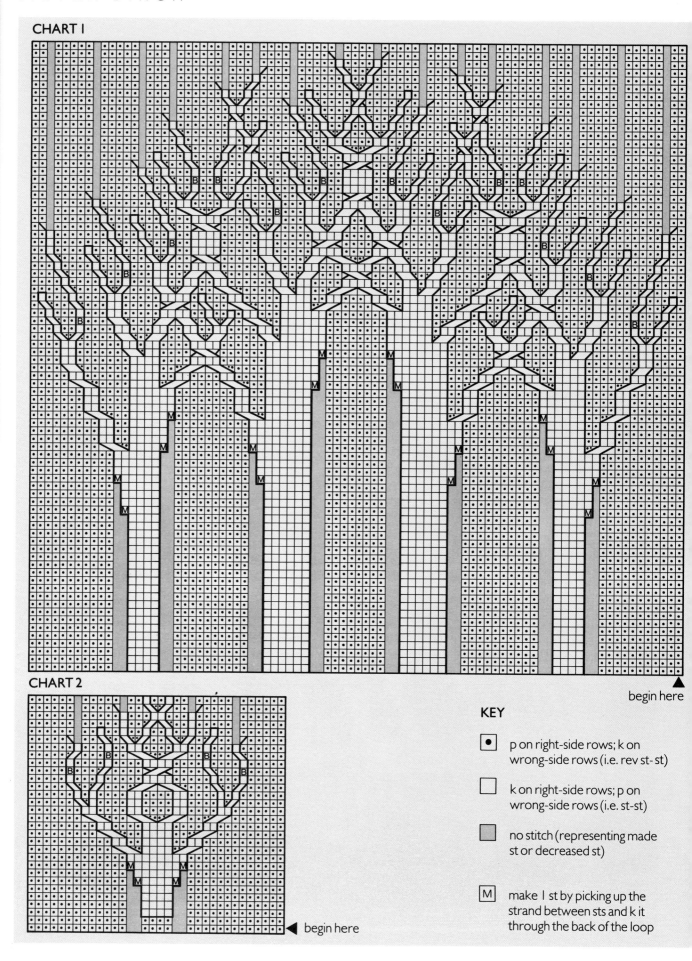

begin here

begin here

**KEY**

- ⊙ p on right-side rows; k on wrong-side rows (i.e. rev st-st)

- ☐ k on right-side rows; p on wrong-side rows (i.e. st-st)

- ▨ no stitch (representing made st or decreased st)

- Ⓜ make 1 st by picking up the strand between sts and k it through the back of the loop

**B** k into back of st

 sl next 2 sts on to cable needle and leave at back of work, k 2 then p 2 from cable needle

 sl next 2 sts on to cable needle and leave at front of work, p 2 then k 2 from cable needle

 sl next st on to cable needle and leave at back of work, k 1 then p st from cable needle

 sl next st on to cable needle and leave at front of work, p 1 then k st from cable needle

 sl next 2 sts on to cable needle and leave at back of work, k 2 then k 2 from cable needle

 sl next 2 sts on to cable needle and leave at front of work, k 2 then k 2 from cable needle

 sl next st on to cable needle and leave at back of work, k 2 then p st from cable needle

 sl next 2 sts on to cable needle and leave at front of work, p 1 then k 2 from cable needle

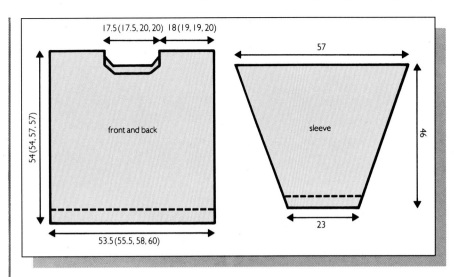 sl next st on to cable needle and leave at back of work, k 1 then k st from cable needle

sl next st on to cable needle and leave at front of work, k 1 then k st from cable needle

 p 2 tog

 sl 1, p 1, pass slipped stitch over

holder, rejoin yarn to inner end of rem 37 (38, 39, 40) sts and k to end. Complete to match 1st side.

## FRONT
Work as back to ***.
Beg with a k row, work 4 rows.

### Neck Shaping
Work as for back but after completing shaping work 8 rows straight instead of 2.

## SLEEVES
With 4 mm needles, cast on 42 sts.
Rib 10 rows as at beg of back.
Change to 5 mm needles.
Cont in patt thus:
**1st row (right side)** K 6, reading row 1 of Chart 2 from right to left work 30 sts, k 6.
**2nd row** P 6, reading row 2 of Chart 2 from left to right work 30 sts, p 6.
**3rd row** K 6, m 1, reading row 3 of Chart 2 from right to left work 30 sts, m 1, k 6.
Cont in this way, working m 1 inside st-st borders at each end of every 3rd row until there are 102 sts, working extra sts in rev st-st – thus 3rd rep of chart has been completed.
**Next row** K 6, p 90, k 6.
**Next row** P 6, k 90, p 6.
Cast off loosely.

## NECKBAND
Join right shoulder seam using 5 mm needle thus: place wrong sides tog and with front facing, cast off both sets of sts tog knit-wise taking 1 st from each needle tog each time.
With right side facing and 4 mm needles, pick up and k 12 sts evenly down left front neck, k across 24 (26, 28, 30) sts at centre front, pick up and k 12 sts up right front neck and 7 sts down right back neck, k across 24 (26, 28, 30) sts at centre back then pick up and k 7 sts up left back neck. 86 (90, 94, 98) sts.
Beg with 2nd rib row, rib 9 rows as at beg of back.
Cast off loosely knit-wise.

## MAKING UP
Join left shoulder as for right shoulder. When joining seams always take 1 st from each side into seam to match ribs. Join neckband seam. Place markers on side edges of back and front 28 cm from shoulder seams. With centre of cast-off edge of sleeves to shoulder seams, sew on sleeves between markers. Press lightly with a barely damp cloth omitting rib. Join side and sleeve seams.

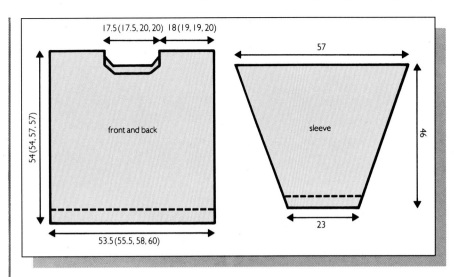

front and back

54 (54, 57, 57)

17.5 (17.5, 20, 20)  18 (19, 19, 20)

53.5 (55.5, 58, 60)

sleeve

57

46

23

STAR GAZER

# STAR GAZER

## NORTHERN LIGHTS

*S*NUGGLE INTO A GIGANTIC, WARM SWEATER, SPLASHED WITH SCANDINAVIAN STARS AND TOP IT WITH A TASSELLED CAP. DESIGNED BY MELODY GRIFFITHS

### MATERIALS
Samband Lopi
5 × 100 g balls yellow, shade 067 (M)
5 × 100 g balls royal, shade 069 (A)
3 × 100 g balls navy, shade 075 (B)
1 × 100 g ball white, shade 001 (C)
Pair each 4½ mm (No 7) and 6½ mm (No 3) knitting needles, use either extra long needles or circular needles

### MEASUREMENTS
One size, to fit up to bust 107 cm, 42 in
Actual measurement – 160 cm, 63 in
Length – 68 cm
Sleeve length – 37 cm

### TENSION
15 sts and 15 rows to 10 cm over patt on 6½ mm needles

### ABBREVIATIONS
beg – beginning; cm – centimetres; cont – continue; dec – decrease; in – inches; inc – increase; k – knit; p – purl; patt – pattern; rem – remaining; rep – repeat; sl – slip; st(s) – stitch(es); st-st – stocking stitch

### NOTE
If using circular needles work forwards and back in rows

NORTHERN LIGHTS

STAR GAZER

## SWEATER
## BACK
With 4½ mm needles and B, cast on
121 sts.
Work 6 rows in k 1, p 1 rib, beg
wrong-side rows p 1.
Change to 6½ mm needles.
P 1 row with A. P 1 row with C.
Cont in st-st from Chart 1 thus:
**1st row (right side)** Reading row 1 of
chart from right to left, k the 20 patt sts
6 times, then k last st of chart.
**2nd row** Reading row 2 of chart from
left to right, p first st of chart then p 20
patt sts 6 times.
**3rd to 29th rows** As 1st and 2nd rows
but working rows 3 to 29 of chart.
*Cont from Chart 2 thus:
**1st row (wrong side)** Reading row 1
of chart from left to right, p first st then
p 40 patt sts 3 times.
**2nd row** Reading row 2 of chart from
right to left, k the 40 patt sts 3 times,
then k last st of chart.
**3rd to 34th rows** As 1st and 2nd rows
but working rows 3 to 34 of chart**.
Rep from * to ** once.
Cast off with M.

## FRONT
Work as back to **.
Cont from Chart 2 and work 1st to
28th rows again.

### Neck Shaping
**Next row** Patt 47 sts, turn.
Keeping patt correct cont on these sts
only for 1st side and leave rem sts on a
spare needle.
Dec 1 st at neck edge on the next 5
rows.
Cast off rem 42 sts with M.
With right side facing, sl centre 27 sts
on to a stitch holder, rejoin yarn to
inner end of rem 47 sts and complete
to match 1st side.

## SLEEVES
With 4½ mm needles and B, cast on
41 sts.
Work 6 rows in k 1, p 1 rib, beg
wrong-side rows p 1.
Change to 6½ mm needles.
P 1 row with A. P 1 row with C.
Cont in st-st from Chart 1 thus:
**1st row (right side)** Reading row 1 of
chart from right to left, k the 20 patt sts
twice, then k last st of chart.
**2nd row** Reading row 2 of chart from
left to right, p first st of chart then p 20
patt sts twice.

**3rd to 29th rows** Increasing 1 st at
each end of every right-side row, work
as set on 1st and 2nd rows but working
rows 3 to 29 of chart, taking extra sts
into patt. 69 sts.
Cont from Chart 3 thus:
**1st row (wrong side)** Reading row 1
of chart from left to right, p first 3 sts of
chart then p 6 patt sts 11 times.
Cont from Chart 3 as set on 1st row,
reading right-side rows from right to
left and inc 1 st at each end of every
right-side row until there are 87 sts
and a total of 19 rows of Chart 3 have
been completed.
**Next row** K with B, inc 1 st at each end
of row.
Cast off the 89 sts with B.

## NECKBAND
Join right shoulder seam.
With right side facing, using 6½ mm
needles and A, pick up and k 9 sts
down left front neck, k across 27 sts at
centre front, pick up and k 8 sts up
right front neck then pick up and k 37
sts across centre 37 sts of back. 81 sts.
Cont in st-st from Chart 1 thus:
**Next row** Reading row 25 of chart
from left to right, p first st of chart, then
p 20 patt sts 4 times.
**Next row** Reading row 26 of chart
from right to left, k 20 patt sts 4 times,
then k last st of chart.
Rep last 2 rows once but work rows
27 and 28 of chart.
P 1 row with A.
Change to 4½ mm needles.
P 1 row with B. With B, work 5 rows in
p 1, k 1 rib, beg right-side rows k 1.
Cast off in rib.

## MAKING UP
Press. Join left shoulder and neckband
seam. With centre of cast-off edge of

sleeves to shoulder seams, sew on
sleeves. Taking ½ st from each edge
into seams, join side and sleeve seams.

## HAT
With 4½ mm needles and B, cast on
81 sts.
Work 6 rows in k 1, p 1 rib, beg
wrong-side rows p 1.
Change to 6½ mm needles.
P 1 row with A. P 1 row with C.
Cont in st-st from Chart 1 thus:
**1st row (right side)** Reading row 1 of
chart from right to left, k the 20 patt sts
4 times, then k last st of chart.
**2nd row** Reading row 2 of chart from
left to right, p first st of chart then p 20
patt sts 4 times.
**3rd to 24th rows** As 1st and 2nd rows
but working rows 3 to 24 of chart.
Cast off with A.

## MAKING UP
Press. Taking ½ st from each edge into
seam, join centre back seam. With
seam to centre, join cast-off edges.
With M, make 2 small tassels and
secure 1 to each end of top seam.

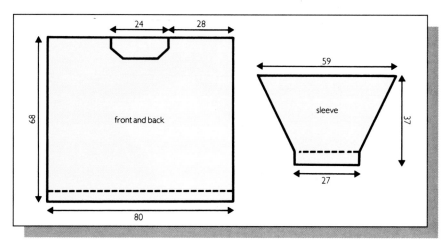

**CHART I**

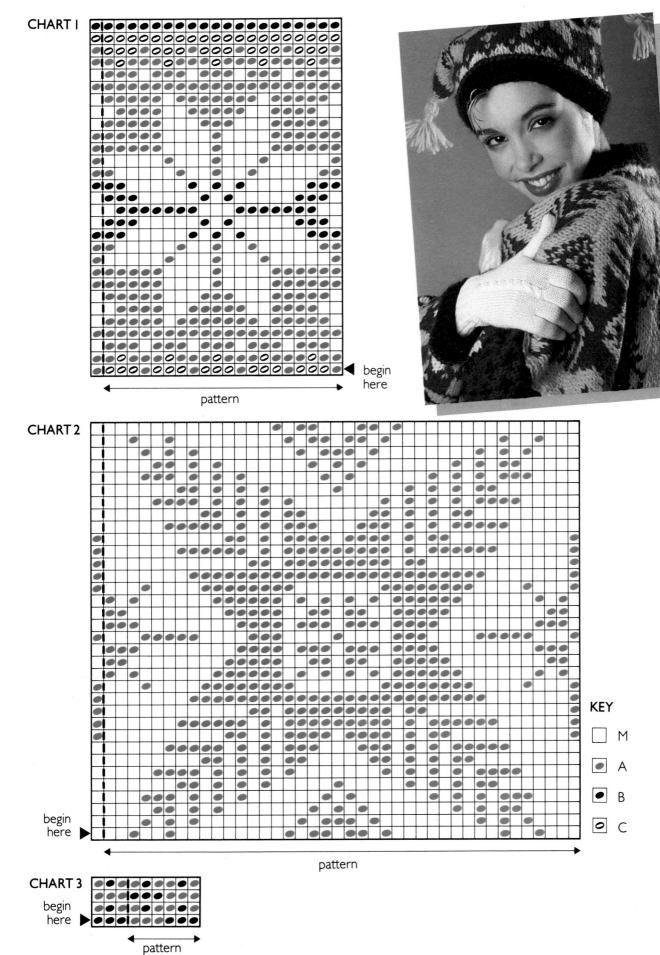

begin
here

pattern

**CHART 2**

begin
here

pattern

**KEY**

☐ M

◑ A

◐ B

⊘ C

**CHART 3**

begin
here

pattern

BROCADE

# BROCADE

## FINE ROMANCE

T HE FABRIC IS A RICH
MIXTURE OF
MOHAIR AND METALLIC
YARN, FALLING IN SOFT
FOLDS. THE STYLE IS
SIMPLE AND RELAXED
ENOUGH TO WEAR
WITH CASUAL
CLOTHES. DESIGNED BY
ZOE HUNT

### MATERIALS
7 × 40 g balls Georges Picaud No 1
Kid Mohair shade 163 (M)
17 × 20 g balls Georges Picaud Feu
d'Artifice shade 14 (A)
Pair each 3¾ mm (No 9) and 4½ mm
(No 7) knitting needles

### MEASUREMENTS
One size, to fit up to bust 97 cm, 38 in
Actual measurement – 125 cm, 49 in
Length – 69 cm
Sleeve length – 44 cm

### TENSION
22 sts and 24 rows to 10 cm measured
over patt on 4½ mm (No 7) needles

### ABBREVIATIONS
alt – alternate; beg – beginning; cm –
centimetres; cont – continue; dec –
decrease; foll – following; in – inches;
inc – increas(e)(ing); k – knit; m 1 –
make 1 st by picking up the strand
between sts and k it through the back
of the loop; p – purl; patt – pattern;
rem – remaining; rep – repeat; st(s) –
stitch(es); st-st – stocking stitch

### BACK
With 3¾ mm needles and M, cast on
120 sts.

Work in k 1, p 1 rib in stripes of 2 rows
M, 4 rows A, 2 rows M, 4 rows A, 2
rows M, 4 rows A and 1 row M.
**Next row** With M, rib 3, m 1, *rib 6,
m 1; rep from * to last 3 sts, rib 3.
140 sts.
Change to 4½ mm needles.
Weaving colour not in use loosely
through every 3rd or 4th st on wrong
side, cont in st-st from chart thus
(noting that chart is in two halves, but
should be read as one):
**1st row (right side)** Reading from right
to left, k row 1 of chart.
**2nd row** Reading from left to right,
p row 2 of chart.
Cont in this way until all 100 rows of
chart have been worked (mark each
end of row 82 to denote beg of
armholes), then rep rows 1 to 50.

### Shoulder and Neck Shaping
Cont from chart taking care to keep
patt correct.
Cast off 16 sts at beg of next 2 rows.
**Next row** Cast off 15 sts, k until there
are 27 sts on right needle, turn.
Cont on these sts only for 1st side and

leave rem sts on a spare needle.
Cast off 12 sts at beg of next row.
Cast off rem 15 sts.
**Next row** With right side facing, cast
off centre 24 sts, patt to end.
Cast off 15 sts at beg of next row and
12 sts on the foll row.
Cast off rem 15 sts.

### FRONT
Work as back until a total of 136 rows
of patt have been worked.

### Neck Shaping
**1st row** Patt 62 sts, turn.
Cont on these sts only for 1st side and
leave rem sts on a spare needle.
Cast off 4 sts at beg of next row, 3 sts
on the foll 2 alt rows and 2 sts on the
next 2 alt rows. Dec 1 st at neck edge
on the next 2 alt rows. 46 sts.

### Shoulder Shaping
Cast off 16 sts at beg of next row and
15 sts on the foll alt row.
Patt 1 row. Cast off rem 15 sts.
**Next row** With right side facing, cast
off centre 16 sts, patt to end.

BROCADE

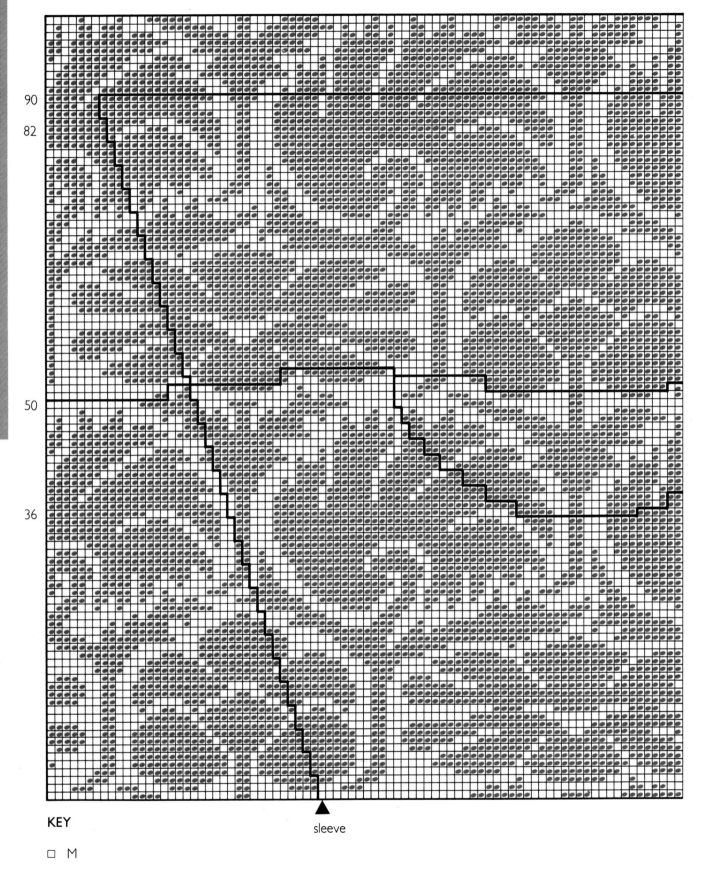

90
82

50

36

**KEY**

□  M

▣  A

▲
sleeve

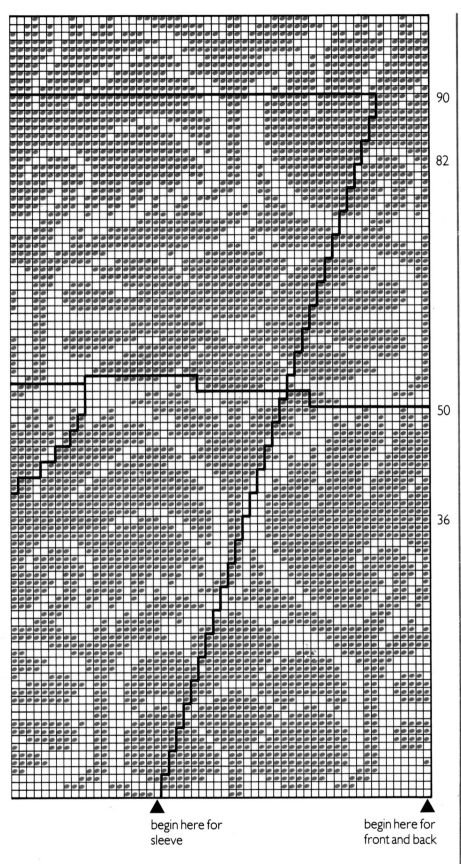

90

82

50

36

▲ begin here for
sleeve

▲ begin here for
front and back

Patt 1 row.
Complete to match 1st side.

## SLEEVES
With 3¾ mm needles and M, cast on
44 sts.
Rib 19 rows as back.
**Next row** With M, inc in first st, m 1,
*rib 2, m 1; rep from * to last st, inc in
last st. 68 sts.
Change to 4½ mm needles.
Working sts indicated, cont from chart,
inc 1 st at each end of 4th row and
every foll 3rd row until there are 126
sts.
Patt 2 rows straight, thus ending with
row 90. Cast off loosely.

## NECKBAND
Join right shoulder seam.
With right side facing, using 3¾ mm
needles and M, pick up and k 70 sts
evenly around front neck and 50 sts
around back neck. 120 sts.
K 1 row.
Cast off knit-wise.

## MAKING UP
Press pieces lightly on wrong side using
a cool iron. Join left shoulder and
neckband seam. With centre of cast-
off edge of sleeves to shoulder seams,
sew on sleeves. Join side and sleeve
seams.

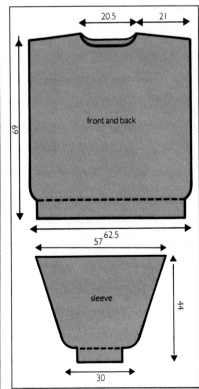

20.5    21

front and back

69

57    62.5

sleeve

44

30

STREET SMART

# STREET SMART

## KNIGHTSBRIDGE

A BIG JACKET OVER A LITTLE SKIRT IS A SMART FORMULA. THE JACKET TAPERS FROM SQUARE SHOULDERS TO A DOUBLE-BREASTED FASTENING AND IS KNITTED IN DOUBLE YARN, WHILE THE MINI IS IN SINGLE YARN. DESIGNED BY GAYE HAWKINS

### MATERIALS
**Jacket**
19 (20) × 50 g balls Poppletons
Emmerdale DK
Pair each 5½ mm (No 5) and 6 mm
(No 4) knitting needles
3 buttons
Shoulder pads

**Skirt**
5 (5) × 50 g balls Poppletons
Emmerdale DK
Pair each 3¾ mm (No 9) and 4 mm
(No 8) knitting needles
Waist length of 2.5 cm wide elastic

### MEASUREMENTS
**Jacket**
To fit bust 86-91 (97-102) cm, 34-36
(38-40) in
Actual measurement – 119 (128) cm,
47 (50½) in
Length – 68 (69) cm
Sleeve length – 41 (42) cm

**Skirt**
To fit hips 91-97 (102-107) cm,
36-38 (40-42) in

*K·N·I·G·H·T·S·B·R·I·D·G·E*

Actual measurement – 93 (99) cm,
36½(39) in
Length – 49 cm
Figures in brackets are for larger size

## TENSION

### Jacket
17 sts and 24 rows to 10 cm over patt
on 6 mm needles using 2 strands of
yarn

### Skirt
26 sts and 32 rows to 10 cm over patt
on 4 mm needles using 1 strand of yarn

## ABBREVIATIONS
alt – alternate; beg – beginning; cm –
centimetres; cont – continue; dec –
decrease; foll – following; g-st – garter
stitch; in – inches; inc – increase; k –
knit; p – purl; patt – pattern; rem –
remain(ing); rep – repeat; sl – slip; st(s)
– stitch(es); st-st – stocking stitch; tog –
together

## JACKET
## BACK
With 5½ mm needles and 2 strands of
yarn, cast on 93 (101) sts.
**1st rib row (right side)** K 1, *p 1, k 1;
rep from * to end.
**2nd rib row** P 1, *k 1, p 1; rep from *
to end.
Rep 1st and 2nd rib rows once.
Change to 6 mm needles.
Cont in patt thus:
**1st row (right side)** P 1, *k 3, p 1; rep
from * to end.
**2nd row** K 2, *p 1, k 3; rep from * to
last 3 sts, p 1, k 2.
These 2 rows form patt for back.
Cont in patt inc 1 st at each end of
every 16th row until there are 103
(111) sts, working inc sts into patt.
Patt 12 rows straight.

### Armhole Shaping
Keeping patt correct, cast off 8 sts at
beg of next 2 rows. Dec 1 st at each
end of every right-side row until 77
(85) sts rem.
Patt 55 (57) rows straight.

### Shoulder Shaping
Cast off 11 (13) sts at beg of next 4
rows. Cast off rem 33 sts.

### POCKET LININGS
**Make 2** With 6 mm needles and 1
strand of yarn, cast on 23 sts.
Work in st-st for 21 cm, ending with a

p row.
Break off yarn and leave sts on a stitch
holder.

### LEFT FRONT
With 5½ mm needles and 2 strands of
yarn, cast on 66 (70) sts.
**1st rib row (right side)** *K 1, p 1; rep
from * to last 6 sts, k 6.
**2nd rib row** K 5, *p 1, k 1; rep from *
to last st, p 1.
Rep 1st and 2nd rib rows once.
Change to 6 mm needles.
Cont in patt thus:
**1st row (right side)** *P 1, k 3; rep from
* to last 6 sts, p 1, k 5.
**2nd row** K 7, *p 1, k 3; rep from * to
last 3 sts, p 1, k 2.
These 2 rows form patt for left front.
Cont in patt inc 1 st at end of every

16th row until there are 69 (73) sts,
working inc sts into patt.
Patt 2 rows straight, thus ending with a
2nd row.
**Pocket Opening row** Patt 6 (10) sts, sl
next 23 sts on to a stitch holder, patt
across sts of one pocket lining, patt 40.
Patt 7 rows straight.
**1st buttonhole row (right side)** Patt
57 (61) sts, cast off next 4 sts, patt to
end.
**2nd buttonhole row** Patt 8, cast on
4 sts, patt to end.
Patt 3 rows straight.
Inc 1 st at end of next row.

### Front Shaping
**1st row (right side)** Patt to last 7 sts,
k 2 tog, k 5.
Patt 2 rows.

**4th row** K 5, k 2 tog, patt to end.
Patt 2 rows.
Inc 1 st at end of 16th row from previous inc, AND AT THE SAME TIME, rep last 6 rows until 61 (65) sts rem, ending with a 4th row.

## Armhole Shaping

Cast off 8 sts at beg of next row, then dec 1 st at armhole edge on the next 5 right-side rows, AND AT THE SAME TIME, dec at front edge as before until 27 (31) sts rem.
Patt 3 (5) rows straight, thus ending at armhole edge.

## Shoulder Shaping

Cast off 11 (13) sts at beg of next row and on the foll alt row.
Work 9.5 cm in g-st on rem 5 sts. Cast off.

## RIGHT FRONT

With 5½ mm needles and 2 strands of yarn, cast on 66 (70) sts.
**1st rib row (right side)** K 6, *p 1, k 1; rep from * to end.
**2nd rib row** *P 1, k 1; rep from * to last 6 sts, p 1, k 5.
Rep 1st and 2nd rib rows once.
Change to 6 mm needles.
Cont in patt thus:
**1st row (right side)** K 5, p 1, *k 3, p 1; rep from * to end.
**2nd row** K 2, p 1, *k 3, p 1; rep from * to last 7 sts, k 7.
These 2 rows form patt for right front.
Cont in patt inc 1 st at beg of every 16th row until there are 69 (73) sts, working inc sts into patt.
Patt 2 rows straight, thus ending with a 2nd row.
**Pocket Opening row** Patt 40, sl next 23 sts on to a stitch holder, patt across sts of pocket lining, patt 6 (10).
Patt 7 rows straight.
**1st buttonhole row (right side)** Patt 8, cast off next 4 sts, patt to end.
**2nd buttonhole row** Patt 57 (61) sts, cast on 4 sts, patt to end.
Patt 3 rows straight.
Inc 1 st at beg of next row.

## Front Shaping

**1st row (right side)** K 5, k 2 tog, patt to end.
Patt 2 rows.
**4th row** Patt to last 7 sts, k 2 tog, k 5.
Patt 2 rows.
Inc 1 st at beg of 16th row from previous inc, AND AT THE SAME

TIME, rep last 6 rows until 61 (65) sts rem, ending with a 4th row.
Patt 1 row.
Complete to match left front from armhole shaping but patt 1 extra row before working shoulder shaping.

## SLEEVES

With 5½ mm needles and 2 strands of yarn, cast on 45 (49) sts.
Rib 4 rows as given at beg of back.
Change to 6 mm needles.
Cont in patt thus:
**1st row (right side)** K 0 (2), *p 1, k 3; rep from * to last 1 (3) sts, p 1, k 0 (2).
This row sets patt.
Working inc sts into patt to match back, *patt 2 rows, inc 1 st at each end of next row, patt 3 rows, inc 1 st at each end of next row*. Rep from * to * until there are 97 (101) sts.
Patt 2 (4) rows straight. •

## Top Shaping

Cast off 8 sts at beg of next 2 rows.
Dec 1 st at each end of next row and every foll alt row until 71 (75) sts rem, then on every row until 23 (27) sts rem. Cast off.

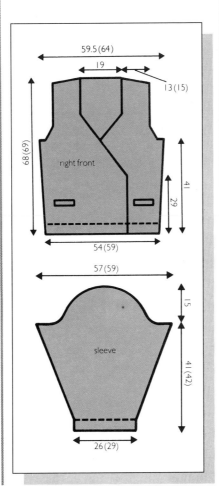

## POCKET TOPS

With right side facing, using 5½ mm needles and 2 strands of yarn, work 4 rows in p 1, k 1 rib across sts on stitch holder. Cast off in rib.

## MAKING UP

Sew down pocket linings on wrong side and sides of pocket tops on right side. Join shoulder seams. Join cast-off edges of back neckbands then sew to back neck. Join side and sleeve seams. Set in sleeves. Sew 1 button to right side of left front to correspond to right front buttonhole. Sew 1 button to wrong side of right front to correspond to left front buttonhole. Sew rem button to right side of right front in the same position as button on wrong side. Sew in shoulder pads.

## SKIRT

## BACK AND FRONT ALIKE

With 3¾ mm needles and 1 strand of yarn, cast on 123 (131) sts.
**1st rib row (right side)** P 1, *k 1, p 1; rep from * to end.
**2nd rib row** K 1, *p 1, k 1; rep from * to end.
Rep 1st and 2nd rib rows 3 times.
Change to 4 mm needles.
Cont in patt thus:
**1st row (right side)** K 3, *p 1, k 3; rep from * to end.
**2nd row** K 1, *p 1, k 3; rep from * to last 2 sts, p 1, k 1.
These 2 rows form patt.
Rep these 2 rows until work measures 28 cm from cast-on edge, ending with a 2nd row.

## Hip Shaping

Keeping patt correct, dec 1 st at each end of next row and every foll 4th row until 91 (99) sts rem. Patt 3 rows straight.
Change to 3¾ mm needles. Rep 1st and 2nd rib rows 5 times. Cast off in rib.

## MAKING UP

Join side seams. Join elastic into ring and attach to wrong side of waist rib using a herringbone casing.

# KENSINGTON

THERE'S AN ESSENTIALLY ENGLISH FEEL ABOUT A LONG SWEATER OVER AN EVEN LONGER SKIRT. DOUBLE WELTS AND CONTRAST EDGINGS ARE DISTINCTIVE FEATURES. DESIGNED BY BRENDA SPARKES

## MATERIALS
### Sweater
14 × 50 g balls Patons Beehive Double Knitting (A)
1 × 50 g ball Patons Beehive Double Knitting (B)
Pair each 3 mm (No 11) and 3¾ mm (No 9) knitting needles
3 mm (No 11) circular knitting needle – 100 cm long
Cable needle

### Skirt
9 × 50 g balls Patons Beehive Double Knitting (A)
1 × 50 g ball Patons Beehive Double Knitting (B)
Pair each 3¼ mm (No 10) and 3¾ mm (No 9) knitting needles
Waist length of 2.5 cm wide elastic

## MEASUREMENTS
### Sweater
One size, to fit up to bust 91 cm, 36 in
Actual measurement – 112 cm, 44 in
Length – 78 cm
Sleeve length – 46 cm

### Skirt
One size, to fit up to hips 97 cm, 38 in
Length – 85 cm

## TENSION
### Sweater
36 sts (1 patt rep) to 11.5 cm and 30 rows to 10 cm over patt on 3¾ mm needles

### Skirt
26 sts to 10 cm measured over slightly stretched rib on 3¾ mm needles

## ABBREVIATIONS

beg – beginning; c 12 – slip next 6 sts on to cable needle and hold at front, k 6 then k 6 from cable needle; cm – centimetres; cont – continue; dec – decrease; in – inches; inc – increase(ing); k – knit; p – purl; patt – pattern; rem – remain(ing); rep – repeat; st(s) – stitch(es); tog – together

## SWEATER
### BACK

**First Welt** With 3 mm needles and B, cast on 120 sts.
Work 1 row in k 2, p 2 rib.
Change to A and cont in k 2, p 2 rib for 6 cm.
Change to B and rib 1 row.
Break yarn and leave sts on a spare needle.
**Second Welt** Work as for first welt but cont in A for 14 cm, then change to B and rib 1 row. Do not break yarn.
**Joining row** Place first welt in front of second welt and with B rib to end working 1 st from each needle tog. 120 sts.
Cont in A.
**Inc row** P 2, *inc in next st, p 1; rep from * to last 2 sts, p 2. 178 sts.
Change to 3¾ mm needles.
Cont in patt thus:

**1st row (right side)** P 2, k 2, *p 1, k 24, p 1, k 2, p 2, k 2, p 2, k 2; rep from * to last 30 sts, p 1, k 24, p 1, k 2, p 2.
**2nd row** K 2, p 2, *k 2, p 22, k 2, p 2, k 2, p 2; rep from * to last 30 sts, k 2, p 22, k 2, p 2, k 2.
**3rd row** P 2, k 2, *p 3, k 20, p 3, k 2, p 2, k 2, p 2; rep from * to last 30 sts, p 3, k 20, p 3, k 2, p 2.
**4th row** K 2, p 2, *k 4, p 18, k 4, p 2, k 2, p 2, k 2; rep from * to last 30 sts, k 4, p 18, k 4, p 2, k 2.
**5th row** P 2, k 2, *p 5, k 2, c 12, k 2, p 5, k 2, p 2, k 2, p 2, k 2; rep from * to last 30 sts, p 5, k 2, c 12, k 2, p 5, k 2, p 2.
**6th row** K 2, p 2, *k 6, p 14, k 6, p 2, k 2, p 2, k 2, p 2; rep from * to last 30 sts, k 6, p 14, k 6, p 2, k 2.
**7th row** P 2, k 2, *p 5, k 16, p 5, k 2, p 2, k 2, p 2, k 2; rep from * to last 30 sts, p 5, k 16, p 5, k 2, p 2.
**8th row** As 4th row.
**9th row** As 3rd row.
**10th row** As 2nd row.
These 10 rows form patt.
Patt straight until back measures 78 cm from cast-on edge of second welt.
Cast off.

## FRONT

Work as back until front measures 53 cm from cast-on edge of second welt, ending with a wrong-side row.

### Neck Shaping

**1st row** Patt 89 sts, turn.
Keeping patt correct, cont on these sts only for 1st side and leave rem sts on a spare needle.
Dec 1 st at neck edge on every right-side row until 58 sts rem.
Patt straight until front matches back to shoulder. Cast off.
**Next row** With right side facing, rejoin A to inner end of 89 sts on spare needle and patt to end.
Complete to match 1st side.

## SLEEVES

With 3 mm needles and B, cast on 56 sts.
Work 1 row in k 2, p 2 rib.
Change to A and cont in rib until sleeve measures 8 cm from cast-on edge.
Change to B and rib 1 row.
**Inc row** *P 3, inc in next st; rep from * to end. 70 sts.
Change to 3¾ mm needles and cont in A.
Work in patt as back, inc 1 st at each end of every 3rd row until there are 142 sts, working inc sts in k 2, p 2 rib.
Patt straight until sleeve measures 46 cm from cast-on edge.
Cast off loosely.

## NECKBAND

Matching sts, join both shoulder seams.
With right side facing, using 3 mm circular needle and B and beg at centre front, pick up and k 92 sts evenly up right front neck, 48 sts across back neck and 92 sts down left front neck. 232 sts.
Work forwards and back in rows.
Work 1 row in k 2, p 2 rib.
Twisting A and B tog on wrong side to prevent holes, cont thus:
**Next row (right side)** K 1 with B, rib to end with A.
**Next row** With A, rib to last st, p 1 with B.
Rep last 2 rows 4 times.
Rib 1 row with B.
Cast off in rib with B.

## MAKING UP

With centre of cast-off edge of sleeves to shoulder seams, sew on sleeves.
Join sleeve seams. Joining the two welts separately, join side seams.
Overlap B end of neckband over other end and sew row-ends neatly to sides of 'V'.

## SKIRT
### BACK

With 3¾ mm needles and B, cast on 142 sts.
**1st rib row (right side)** K 2, *p 2, k 2; rep from * to end.
Cont in A.
**2nd rib row** P 2, *k 2, p 2; rep from * to end.
Rep last 2 rows until work measures 85 cm from cast-on edge, ending with a wrong-side row.
Change to 3¼ mm needles.
Rib 10 rows.
Cast off loosely in rib.

## FRONT

Work as for back.

## MAKING UP

Join side seams. Join elastic into ring and attach to wrong side of waist rib using a herringbone casing.

front and back

18.5
78
53
14
56
45

sleeve

46
22

# BELGRAVIA

**M**ORE THAN A LONG SWEATER – THIS DRESS FORMS A SLEEK WEDGE, WIDENING OUT INTO BIG SHOULDERS WITH UNUSUAL RAGLAN AND SADDLE SHAPING. DESIGNED BY BRENDA SPARKES

## MATERIALS
2 (3, 3) × 500 g cones Rowan Light Weight DK
Pair each 3¼ mm (No 10) and 4 mm (No 8) knitting needles
3 mm (No 11) circular knitting needle, 40 cm long
Raglan shoulder pads

## MEASUREMENTS
To fit bust 86 (91, 97) cm, 34 (36, 38) in
Actual measurement – 113 (119, 125) cm, 44½ (47, 49) in
Length – 93 (95, 97) cm
Sleeve length – 41 (42, 43) cm
Figures in brackets are for larger sizes

## TENSION
25 sts and 42 rows to 10 cm measured over patt on 4 mm (No 8) needles

## ABBREVIATIONS
beg – beginning; cm – centimetres; cont– continue; dec –decrease; foll – following; in – inches; inc – increas(ed)(ing); k – knit; p – purl; patt – pattern; rem – remain(ing); rep – repeat; sl – slip; sl 1 p – slip 1 stitch purlwise; st(s) – stitch(es); tbl – through back of loop(s); tog – together; yfwd – yarn forward

## BACK
With 3¼ mm needles, cast on 105 (113, 121) sts.
**1st rib row (right side)** K 2, *p 1, k 1; rep from * to last st, k 1.
**2nd rib row** K 1, *p 1, k 1; rep from * to end.
Rep 1st and 2nd rib row for 2 cm, ending with a 2nd rib row.
Change to 4 mm needles.

STREET SMART

Cont in patt thus:

**1st row (right side)** K 2, *yfwd, sl 1 p, leave yarn at front, k 1; rep from * to last st, k 1.

**2nd row** K 1, *p 1, k the slipped st and the made st tog; rep from * to last 2 sts, p 1, k 1.

These 2 rows form patt.

Cont in patt, inc 1 st at each end of 15th row and every foll 14th row until there are 141 (149, 157) sts, working inc sts into patt.

Patt straight until work measures 66 cm from cast-on edge, ending with a wrong-side row.

### Raglan Shaping

Dec 1 st at each end of every right-side row until 47 sts rem, ending with a wrong-side row.

Cast off loosely.

### FRONT

Work as back until 61 sts rem, ending with a wrong-side row.

### Neck Shaping

**1st row** K 2 tog, patt 18 sts, turn.

Cont on these 19 sts only for 1st side and leave rem sts on a spare needle. Keeping patt correct, cont to dec at raglan edge on every right-side row, AND AT THE SAME TIME, dec 1 st at neck edge on the next 11 rows. 3 sts. Dec 1 st at raglan edge on the next

row. Patt 1 row.

K 2 tog and fasten off.

**Next row** With right side facing, sl centre 21 sts on to a stitch holder, rejoin yarn to inner end of rem 20 sts, patt 18, K 2 tog.

Complete to match 1st side.

### LEFT SLEEVE

With 3¼ mm needles, cast on 51 (55, 59) sts.

Rib 8 cm as given at beg of back, ending with a 2nd rib row.

Change to 4 mm needles.

Cont in patt, inc 1 st at each end of every 4th row until there are 105 (107, 109) sts, then on every foll 3rd row until there are 119 (127, 135) sts, working inc sts into patt.

Patt straight until sleeve measures 41 (42, 43) cm from cast-on edge, ending with a wrong-side row.

### Raglan Shaping

**1st row** Rib 46 (50, 54), k 2 tog, rib 23, k 2 tog tbl, rib 46 (50, 54).

**2nd row** Patt to end.

**3rd row** Rib 45 (49, 53), k 2 tog, rib 23, k 2 tog tbl, rib 45 (49, 53).

**4th row** As 2nd.

**5th row** Rib 44 (48, 52), k 2 tog, rib 23, k 2 tog tbl, rib 44 (48, 52).

Cont to dec in this way, keeping centre 27 sts as set and working 1 st less at each end on every successive right-side row until 25 sts rem, ending with a wrong-side row.

### Saddle Shaping

**1st row** Patt 13 sts, turn.

Cont on these sts only for saddle extension and leave rem 12 sts on a safety pin.

Work in patt for 9.5 cm, ending with a wrong-side row.

Cast off loosely.

### RIGHT SLEEVE

Work to match left sleeve but end with a right-side row before working saddle shaping.

### COLLAR

Join raglan seams. Join cast-off edges of saddle extensions at top of sleeves. Join saddle extensions to cast-off sts at top of back. Join side and sleeve seams.

**Note** on 1st row of collar, when working across sts on safety pin on right sleeve, p the slipped st and the made st tog each time.

**1st row** With right side facing and using 3 mm circular knitting needle, pick up and k 27 sts across right saddle extension and 28 sts across left saddle extension, work in p 1, k 1 rib across sts on safety pin, pick up and k 18 sts evenly down left front neck, work in p 1, k 1 rib across sts at centre front, pick up and k 18 sts up right front neck, work in k 1, p 1 rib across sts on safety pin. 136 sts.

Work in rounds of k 1, p 1 rib for 14 cm. Cast off loosely in rib.

Sew in shoulder pads.

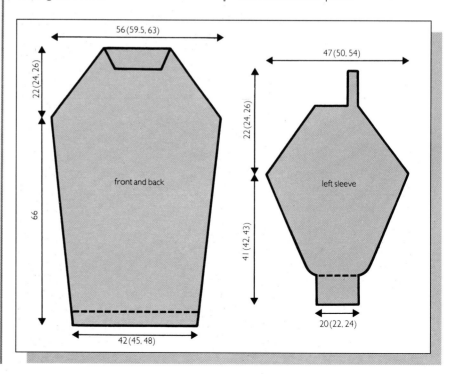

56(59.5, 63)

22(24, 26)

66

front and back

42(45, 48)

47(50, 54)

22(24, 26)

41(42, 43)

left sleeve

20(22, 24)

# SKI GRAPHIQUE

# SKI GRAPHIQUE

## SUPERSAMPLER

*S*WEATER, HOOD
AND COWL ADD
UP TO A MONTAGE OF
CRISP CONTRASTING
AND COMPLEMENTARY
PATTERNS. THE
GRAPHICS AND SIZING
WOULD MAKE IT A
GREAT SWEATER FOR A
MAN, TOO. DESIGNED
BY MARY NORDEN

### MATERIALS
Wendy Shetland Double Knit
**Sweater**
6 × 50 g balls Tiree (M)
4 × 50 g balls Rhum (A)
3 × 50 g balls Othello (B)
2 × 50 g balls Barra (C)
2 × 50 g balls White Heather (D)
**Cowl**
2 × 50 g balls Othello (B)
2 × 50 g balls White Heather (D)
**Hood**
2 × 50 g balls White Heather (D)
2 × 50 g balls Herma Ness (E)
Pair each 3 mm (No 11) and 3¾ mm
(No 9) knitting needles for sweater
and hood
4½ mm (No 7) circular knitting needle,
60 cm long for cowl

### MEASUREMENTS
**Sweater**
To fit up to bust 107 cm, 42 in
Actual measurement – 118 cm, 46½ in
approx
Length – 71 cm approx
Sleeve length – 47 cm approx
**Cowl**
Length – 54 cm
**Hood**
Length – 58 cm

### TENSION
26 sts and 26 rows to 10 cm over st-st
Fair Isle on 3¾ mm needles
22 sts and 30 rows to 10 cm over st-st
on 4½ mm needles

### ABBREVIATIONS
alt – alternate; beg – beginning; cm –

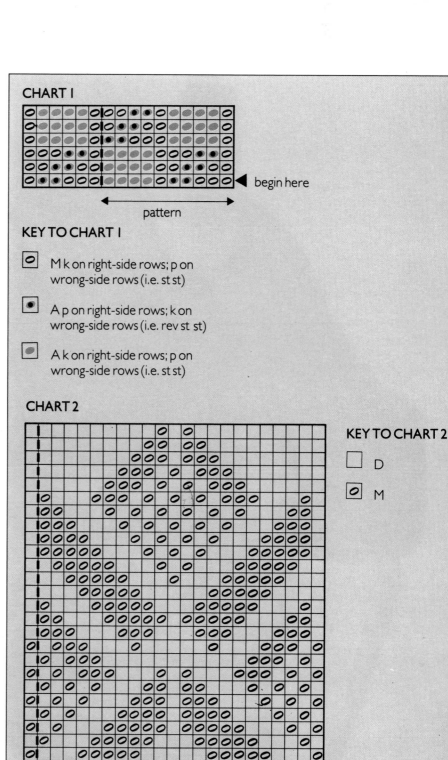

**CHART I**

begin here

pattern

**KEY TO CHART I**

M k on right-side rows; p on
wrong-side rows (i.e. st st)

A p on right-side rows; k on
wrong-side rows (i.e. rev st st)

A k on right-side rows; p on
wrong-side rows (i.e. st st)

**CHART 2**

**KEY TO CHART 2**

☐ D

M

begin here

pattern

## CHART 3

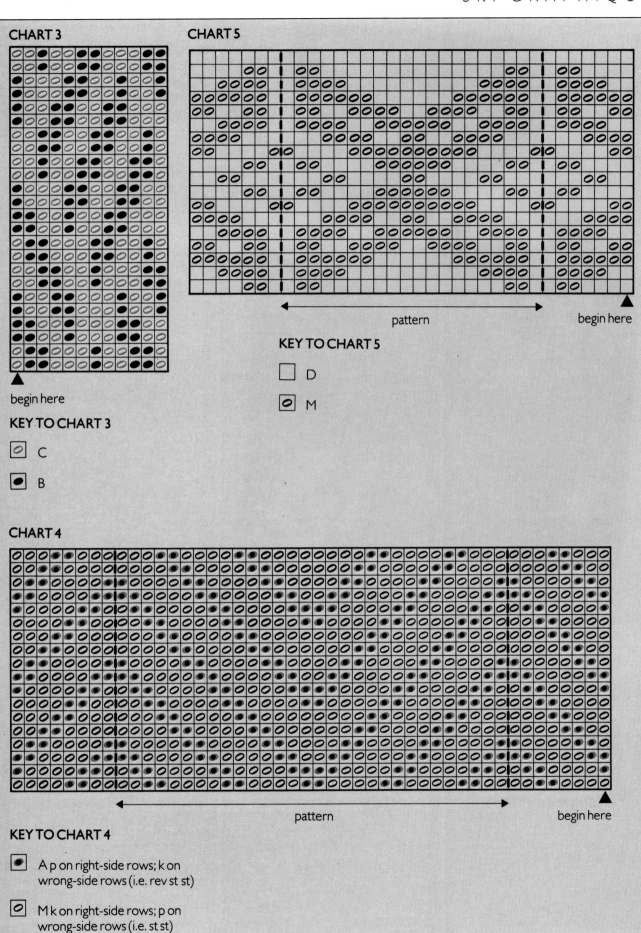

begin here

## KEY TO CHART 3

C

B

## CHART 5

pattern

begin here

## KEY TO CHART 5

D

M

## CHART 4

pattern

begin here

## KEY TO CHART 4

A p on right-side rows; k on wrong-side rows (i.e. rev st st)

M k on right-side rows; p on wrong-side rows (i.e. st st)

*SUPERSAMPLER*

# SKI GRAPHIQUE

centimetres; cont – continue; dec – decrease; foll – following; in – inches; inc – increase; k – knit; p – purl; patt – pattern; rem – remaining; rep – repeat; st(s) – stitch(es); st-st – stocking stitch

## BACK

With 3 mm needles and M, cast on 156 sts.

Work 3 cm in k 1, p 1 rib.

Change to 3¾ mm needles.

Cont from Chart 1 thus:

**1st row (right side)** Reading row 1 of chart from right to left, work 10 patt sts 15 times, then work last 6 sts of chart.

**2nd row** Reading row 2 of chart from left to right, work first 6 sts of chart, then work 10 patt sts 15 times.

**3rd to 6th rows** As 1st and 2nd rows but working rows 3 to 6 of chart.

Rep 1st to 6th rows until work measures approx 35 cm from cast-on

edge, ending with a 6th row.

*K 1 row B. P 1 row D*. Rep from * to * twice, dec 1 st at end of last row. 155 sts.

Cont in st-st from Chart 2 thus:

**1st row (right side)** Reading row 1 of chart from right to left, k 22 patt sts 7 times, then k last st of chart.

**2nd row** Reading row 2 of chart from left to right, p first st of chart, then p 22 patt sts 7 times.

**3rd to 38th rows** As 1st and 2nd rows but working rows 3 to 38 of chart. Inc 1 st at beg of 1st row, work from * to * twice, then k 1 row B. 156 sts.

Cont in st-st from Chart 3 thus:

**1st row (wrong side)** Reading row 1 of chart from left to right, p 12 sts of chart 13 times.

**2nd row** Reading row 2 of chart from right to left, k 12 sts of chart 13 times.

**3rd to 24th rows** As 1st and 2nd rows but working rows 3 to 24 of chart **.

Rep 1st to 15th rows of Chart 3.

### Neck Shaping

**Next row (right side)** Working as row 16 of Chart 3, patt 66, cast off next 24 sts, patt to end.

Keeping patt correct, cont on last set of 66 sts only for 1st side and leave rem sts on a spare needle. Patt 1 row.

***Cast off 6 sts at beg of next row and on the foll alt row. Patt 1 row.

Cast off rem 54 sts.

With wrong side facing, rejoin yarn to inner end of 66 sts on spare needle and complete to match 1st side from *** but patt 2 rows not 1 before casting off.

## FRONT

Work as back to **.

Rep 1st to 5th rows of Chart 3.

### Neck Shaping

**Next row (right side)** Working as row 6 of Chart 3, patt 69, cast off next 18 sts, patt to end.

Keeping patt correct, cont on last set of 69 sts only for 1st side and leave rem sts on a spare needle. Patt 1 row.

****Cast off 5 sts at beg of next row, 3 sts on the foll alt row and 2 sts on the next 2 alt rows. Dec 1 st at beg of next 3 alt rows. Patt 1 row.

Cast off rem 54 sts.

With wrong side facing, rejoin yarn to inner end of sts on spare needle and complete to match 1st side from **** but patt 2 rows not 1 before casting off.

## SLEEVES

With 3 mm needles and M, cast on 64 sts.

Work 7 cm in k 1, p 1 rib.

**Inc row** Rib 4, *inc in next st, rib 4; rep from * to end. 76 sts.

Change to 3¾ mm needles.

**Note** When increasing always take increased sts into patt.

Cont from Chart 4 thus:

**1st row (right side)** Reading row 1 of chart from right to left, patt first 8 sts of chart, work 30 patt sts twice, then patt last 8 sts of chart.

**2nd row** Reading row 2 of chart from left to right, patt first 8 sts of chart, work 30 patt sts twice, then patt last 8 sts of chart. Beg with row 3, cont from chart in this way, inc 1 st at each end of next row and every foll 3rd row until there are 108 sts, thus ending with row

## CHART 6

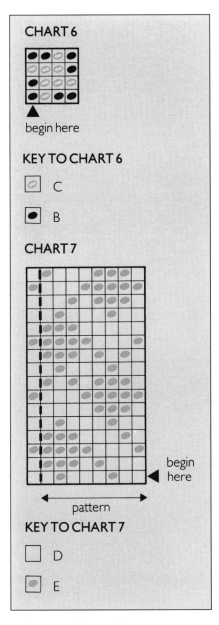

▲
begin here

## KEY TO CHART 6

⊘  C

⬤  B

## CHART 7

begin here ◀

← pattern →

## KEY TO CHART 7

□  D

⊘  E

12 of chart.

Work from * to * of back 3 times, but inc 1 st at each end of every p row. 114 sts.

Cont in st-st from Chart 5 thus:

**1st row (right side)** Reading row 1 of chart from right to left, k first 7 sts of chart, k 20 patt sts 5 times, then k last 7 sts of chart.

Work rows 2 to 18 of chart in this way, inc 1 st at each end of every p row. 132 sts. K 1 row B.

**Next row** With D, inc in first st, p to last st, inc in last st.

Rep last 2 rows once, then k 1 row B. 136 sts.

Cont in st-st from Chart 6 thus:

**1st row (wrong side)** With B, inc in first st, p 1 B, reading row 1 of chart from left to right, p 4 sts of chart to last 2 sts, p 1 B, with C inc in last st.

**2nd row** K 2 C, 1 B, reading row 2 of chart from right to left, k 4 sts of chart to last 3 sts, k 3 C.

**3rd row** With C inc in first st, k 1 C, k 1 B, reading row 3 of chart from left to right, p 4 sts of chart to last 3 sts, p 2 C, with C inc in last st.

**4th row** Reading row 4 of chart from right to left, k 4 sts of chart to end. Cont to inc on every p row in this way until there are 164 sts. Patt 1 row, thus ending with row 4 of chart. Cast off loosely.

## NECKBAND

Join right shoulder seam.

With right side facing, using 3 mm needles and M, pick up and K 62 sts evenly around front neck and 56 sts around back neck. 118 sts.

Work 15 rows in k 1, p 1 rib.

Cast off loosely in rib.

## MAKING UP

Press. Join left shoulder and neckband seam. Fold neckband in half on to wrong side and catch stitch loosely in place. With centre of cast-off edge of sleeves to shoulder seams, sew on sleeves. Join side and sleeve seams.

## COWL

With 4½ mm circular needle and B, cast on 146 sts.

Work throughout in stripes of 1 row D and 1 row B.

Rib 4 rounds.

Cont in st-st (every round k) until work measures 52 cm from cast-on edge, ending with 1 round in B.

Rib 4 rounds.

Cast off in rib with D.

## HOOD

With 3 mm needles and D, cast on 153 sts.

Work 7 cm in k 1, p 1 rib, beg alt rows p 1.

Change to 3¾ mm needles.

Cont in st-st from Chart 7 thus:

**1st row (right side)** Reading row 1 of chart from right to left, k 8 patt sts to last st, then k last st of chart.

**2nd row** Reading row 2 of chart from left to right, p first st of chart, then p 8 patt sts to end.

**3rd to 16th rows** As 1st and 2nd rows but working rows 3 to 16 of chart.

Rep 1st to 16th rows 7 times.

Change to 3 mm needles.

With E, rib 5 rows.

Cast off in rib with E.

Join seam.

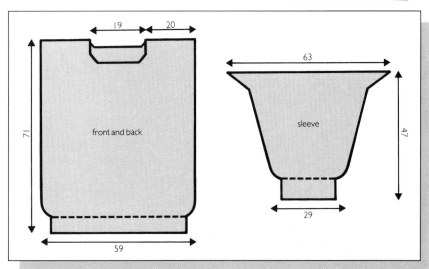

front and back

sleeve

# CAFE SOCIETY

## CRIMSON

W**HEN AN
OTHERWISE
SPORTY STYLE IS
KNITTED IN HEAVY,
SHINY, VISCOSE RIBBON
THE RESULT IS A
DAZZLING EVENING
TRANSFORMATION.
DESIGNED BY
KATE JONES**

### MATERIALS
21 × 50 g balls Pingouin Ruban
Pair each 5½ mm (No 5), 7 mm (No 2)
and 8 mm (No 0) knitting needles
Cable needle

### MEASUREMENTS
One size, to fit up to bust 97 cm, 38 in
Actual measurement – 126 cm,
49½ in approx
Length – 60 cm
Sleeve length – 41 cm

### TENSION
13 sts and 17 rows to 10 cm measured
over st-st on 8 mm needles

### NOTE
In wear, tension of garment may differ,
thus measurements may vary slightly
from those above

### ABBREVIATIONS
alt – alternate; approx – approximate;
beg – beginning; c 3 b – sl next st on to
cable needle and hold at back, k 2 then
k 1 from cable needle; c 3 f – sl next 2
sts on to cable needle and hold at front,
k 1 then k 2 from cable needle; cm –
centimetres; cont – continue; foll –
following; g-st – garter stitch; in –
inches; inc – increase; k – knit; k 1 b –

knit into st 1 row below next st on left
needle and allow st above to drop off
needle; p – purl; patt – pattern; rem –
remaining; rep – repeat; sl – slip; st(s) –
stitch(es); st-st – stocking stitch
Work instructions in square brackets
the number of times given

### BACK
With 7 mm needles, cast on 85 sts.
Work 4 rows in g-st.
Change to 8 mm needles.
Cont in zig-zag patt thus:
**1st row (right side)** K.
**2nd and every foll alt row** P.

**3rd row** K 33, [c 3 f, k 3] twice, c 3 f,
k 37.
**5th row** K 34, [c 3 f, k 3] twice, c 3 f,
k 36.
**7th row** K 35, [c 3 f, k 3] twice, c 3 f,
k 35.
**9th row** K 36, [c 3 f, k 3] twice, c 3 f,
k 34.
**11th row** K 37, [c 3 f, k 3] twice, c 3 f,
k 33.
**13th row** K.
**15th row** K 37, [c 3 b, k 3] twice, c 3 b,
k 33.
**17th row** K 36, [c 3 b, k 3] twice, c 3 b,
k 34.

# C·R·I·M·S·O·N

**19th row** K 35, [c 3 b, k 3] twice, c 3 b, k 35.
**21st row** K 34, [c 3 b, k 3] twice, c 3 b, k 36.
**23rd row** K 33, [c 3 b, k 3] twice, c 3 b, k 37.
**24th row** P.
These 24 rows form patt.
Rep 1st to 24th rows twice, then work 1st to 16th rows again.

### Neck Shaping

**1st row (right side)** K 36, cast off next 13 sts, k to end.
Cont in st-st on last set of 36 sts for 1st side. Leave rem sts on a spare needle. P 1 row.
** Cast off 4 sts at beg of next row, 2 sts on the foll 2 alt rows and 1 st on the next alt row. 27 sts. Work 2 rows straight. Cast off loosely.
**Next row** With wrong side facing, rejoin yarn to inner end of 36 sts on spare needle and complete to match 1st side from ** but work 3 rows straight not 2.

## FRONT

Work as back until a total of 3 complete patts have been worked, then work 1st to 12th rows again.

### Neck Shaping

**1st row (right side)** K 36, cast off next 13 sts, K to end.
Cont in st-st on last set of 36 sts for 1st side. Leave rem sts on a spare needle. P 1 row.
*** Cast off 2 sts at beg of next row and on the foll 3 alt rows, then 1 st on the next alt row. 27 sts.
Work 4 rows straight. Cast off loosely.
**Next row** With wrong side facing, rejoin yarn to inner end of 36 sts on spare needle and complete to match 1st side from *** but work 5 rows straight not 4.

## SLEEVES

With 7 mm needles, cast on 30 sts.
Work 2 rows in g-st.
Change to 8 mm needles.
Cont in st-st, inc 1 st at each end of every 3rd row until there are 72 sts.
Cont straight until sleeve measures 41 cm from cast-on edge.
Cast off very loosely using a size larger needle.

## COLLAR

Joint right shoulder seam.

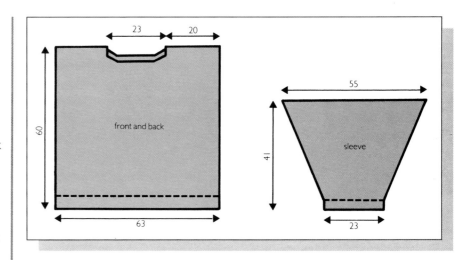

With right side facing and using 5½ mm needles, pick up and k 32 sts evenly around front neck and 30 sts around back neck. 62 sts. P 1 row.
**Patt row** *K 1, k 1 b; rep from * to last 2 sts, k 2.
Rep patt row until collar measures 32 cm. Cast off loosely in patt.

## MAKING UP

Press very lightly.
Join left shoulder and collar seam, reversing collar seam for last 20 cm to allow for turn-over. With centre of cast-off edge of sleeves to shoulder seams, sew on sleeves. Join side and sleeve seams.

# SCARLET

SMOOTH LINES AND CHEVRON STITCHES MAKE THIS THE PERFECT PARTY-GOER, MOVING AND GLITTERING IN THE LIGHT. DESIGNED BY AILEEN SWAN

## MATERIALS

21 (23, 25) × 25 g balls Twilleys Goldfingering
2¾ mm (No 12) and 3 mm (No 11) circular knitting needles, 100 cm long
Cable needle
4 circular or extra long needles, size 3 mm or less, to be used for shoulder and upper sleeve stitch holders
7 small buttons

## MEASUREMENTS

To fit bust 86 (91, 97) cm, 34 (36, 38) in
Actual measurement – 103 (108, 112) cm, 40½ (42½, 44) in
Length – 63 (64, 65) cm
Sleeve length – 45 cm
Figures in brackets are for larger sizes

## TENSION

34 sts and 44 rows to 10 cm over patt on 3 mm needles

## ABBREVIATIONS

alt – alternate; beg – beginning; cm – centimetres; cont – continue; dec – decrease; foll – following; in – inches; inc – increase; k – knit; p – purl; patt – pattern; psso – pass slipped stitch over; rem – remain(ing); rep – repeat; rev st-st – reverse stocking stitch; sl – slip; st(s) – stitch(es); st-st – stocking stitch

## NOTE

Work forwards and back in rows throughout.

## BACK

With 2¾ mm needle, cast on 174 (182, 190) sts.
**1st rib row (right side)** K 2, *p 2, k 2; rep from * to end.
**2nd rib row** P 2, *k 2, p 2; rep from * to end.

Rep 1st and 2nd rib rows 3 times, then work 1st rib row again.
Change to 3 mm needle.
Cont from chart thus (noting that chart is in two halves, but should be read as one):
**1st row (wrong side)** Reading chart from left to right, beg at left-hand line for 1st (2nd, 3rd) size and work 3 (7, 11) sts to dotted line A, work 21 sts between dotted lines A and B 3 times, then work 21 sts between lines B and C once**, now *** work 21 sts

between lines C and D once, then work 21 sts between lines D and E 3 times, work 3 (7, 11) sts beyond line E, thus ending at line for 1st (2nd, 3rd) size.
**2nd row** Reading chart from right to left, beg at right-hand line for 1st (2nd, 3rd) size and work 3 (7, 11) sts to line E, work 21 sts between lines E and D 3 times, then work 21 sts between lines D and C once**, now *** work 21 sts between lines C and B once, work 21 sts between lines B and A 3 times,

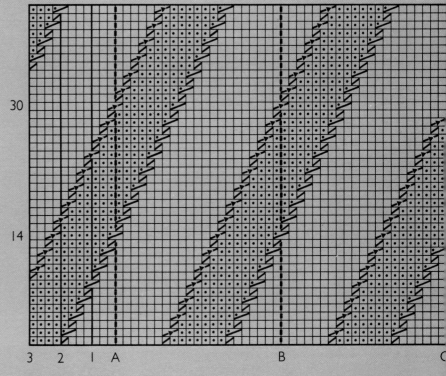

30

14

3   2   1  A                              B                         C

begin here for back
and right front

## KEY

☐ k on right-side rows; p on wrong-side rows (i.e. st st)

⊡ p on right-side rows; k on wrong-side rows (i.e. rev st-st)

⧄ sl st purlwise keeping yarn on wrong side of work

◤ sl 1st st (sl st of previous row) on to cable needle and leave at front of work, k 2nd st then k st from cable needle

◿ sl 1st st (sl st of previous row) on to cable needle and leave at front of work, p 2nd st then k st from cable needle

◺ sl 1st st on to cable needle and leave at back of work, k 2nd st (sl st of previous row) then p st from cable needle

◥ sl 1st st on to cable needle and leave at back of work, k 2nd st (sl st of previous row) then k st from cable needle

work 3 (7, 11) sts beyond line A, thus ending at line for 1st (2nd, 3rd) size. Cont working each row of chart in this way (see note for 14th and 30th rows) until all 42 rows of chart have been completed. These 42 rows form patt. Beg again at 1st row and cont in patt until the 39th row of the 4th patt from beg has been completed. Work should measure 39 cm from beg.

## Sleeve Shaping
Taking extra sts into patt at each side as they occur, cast on 5 sts at beg of next 54 rows. 444 (452, 460) sts.
Cont in patt until the 9th (13th, 17th) row of the 7th patt from beg has been completed.
Work should measure 61 (62, 63) cm from beg.

## Neck Shaping
**1st row** Patt 201 (204, 207) sts, turn. Cont on these sts only for 1st side. Cast off 5 sts at beg of next row and on the foll alt row.

Patt 2 rows. Leave rem 191 (194, 197) sts on a stitch holder.
**Next row** With right side facing, rejoin yarn to inner end of rem sts, cast off centre 42 (44, 46) sts, patt to end. 201 (204, 207) sts.
Cast off 5 sts at beg of next 2 alt rows. Patt 1 row.
Leave rem 191 (194, 197) sts on a stitch holder.

## POCKET LININGS
**Make 2** With 3 mm needle, cast on 38 sts.
Beg k, work 44 rows in st-st.
Break off yarn and leave sts on a stitch holder.

## LEFT FRONT
With 2¾ mm needle, cast on 87 (91, 95) sts.
**1st rib row (right side)** *K 2, p 2; rep from * to last 3 sts, k 3.
**2nd rib row** K 1, p 2, *k 2, p 2; rep from * to end.
Rep 1st and 2nd rib rows 3 times.
**Next row** Inc in 1st st, rib to end. 88 (92, 96) sts.
Change to 3 mm needle.
Cont from chart thus:
**1st row (wrong side)** K 1, reading chart from left to right, work as 1st row of back from *** to end.
**2nd row** Work as 2nd row of back to **, k 1.
Cont in patt in this way, with 1 k st at front edge, until the 11th row of the 2nd patt from beg has been worked.
**Pocket Opening row** Patt 32 (34, 36) sts, sl next 38 sts on to a stitch holder, patt 38 sts of 1 pocket lining, patt 18 (20, 22) sts.
Cont in patt until the 35th row of the 3rd patt from beg has been worked.

## Front Shaping
**1st row** Patt to last 3 sts, k 2 tog, k 1.
Keeping patt correct, cont to dec 1 st in this way at end of every foll 4th row until the 39th row of the 4th patt from beg has been worked. 76 (80, 84) sts.

## Sleeve Shaping
Cont to dec at front edge as set, AND AT THE SAME TIME, cast on 5 sts at beg of next row and on the foll 26 alt rows, taking sts into patt as they occur. 198 (202, 206) sts.
Now dec at neck edge on 6th row from last dec and every foll 6th row until 191 (194, 197) sts rem.

C     D     E   1   2   3

begin here for left front

## NOTE
On 14th and 30th rows of chart dotted lines cut through twist st symbols but this does not change the method of working the twists.
Reading from the right, at dotted line E the 1st half of the twist is shown before the line and the 2nd half after; in the same way in the repeated section between dotted lines E and D, the 1st half of the twist is shown before dotted line D and the 2nd half on the next repeat after dotted line E. Similarly, at the left-hand side of the chart the 1st half of the twist is before dotted line B and the 2nd half after; in the repeated section between dotted lines B and A, the 1st half of the twist is shown before dotted line A and the 2nd half on the next repeat after dotted line B.

Patt straight until the 15th (19th, 23rd) row of the 7th patt from beg has been worked. Leave sts on a stitch holder.

### RIGHT FRONT

With 2¾ mm needle, cast on 87 (91, 95) sts.

**1st row rib (right side)** K 3, *p 2, k 2; rep from * to end.

**2nd rib row** *P 2, k 2; rep from * to last 3 sts, p 2, k 1.

Rep 1st and 2nd rib rows 3 times.

**Next row** Rib to last st, inc in last st. 88 (92, 96) sts.

Change to 3 mm needle.

Cont from chart thus:

**1st row (wrong side)** Work as 1st row of back to **, k 1.

**2nd row** K 1, reading chart from right to left, work as 2nd row of back from *** to end.

Cont in patt as set and complete to match left front, reversing pocket opening row by reading from end to beg; reversing front shapings by working dec as sl 1, k 1, psso at beg instead of end of rows and reversing

sleeve shaping by working 1 row more before sleeve shaping.

### SHOULDER SEAMS

With right sides of right back and right front tog and stitch holder needles parallel, with 3 mm needle, beg at end of sleeve and k 1 st from each needle tog, AND AT THE SAME TIME, cast off to end.

Work left back and left front seam in the same way.

### FRONT BAND

With right side facing and using 2¾ mm needle, pick up and k 104 sts evenly up straight edge of right front, 140 (144, 148) sts up shaped edge to shoulder, 66 (66, 70) sts around back neck, 140 (144, 148) sts down shaped edge of left front and 104 sts down straight edge of left front. 554 (562, 574) sts.

Beg with 1st rib row of back, rib 3 rows.

**Buttonhole row** P 2, k 2, cast off 2 sts, *rib 14 including st rem on needle after casting off, cast off 2 sts; rep from * 5 times, rib to end.

**Next row** Rib to end, casting on 2 sts over each cast-off group. Rib 3 rows. Cast off evenly in rib.

### CUFFS

With right side facing and using 2¾ mm needle, pick up and k 78 (82, 86) sts evenly across straight edge of sleeve.

**Dec row** P 0 (0, 2), k 0 (2, 2), p 1, p 2 tog, *k 2, p 1, p 2 tog; rep from * 14 times, k 0 (2, 2), p 0 (0, 2). 62 (66, 70) sts.

Beg with 1st (2nd, 1st) rib row of back, work in rib for 5 cm. Cast off loosely.

### POCKET TOPS

With right side facing, sl sts of pocket onto 2¾ mm needle.

Beg with 1st rib row of back, rib 7 rows. Cast off loosely in rib.

### MAKING UP

Press lightly. Join side and sleeve seams. Sew on buttons. Sew down pocket linings and sides of pocket tops.

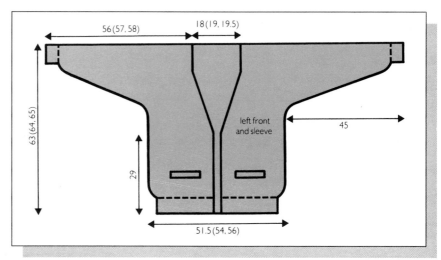

# VERMILION

A PLUNGING SHAWL COLLAR MAKES IMMEDIATE IMPACT, WHILE CABLED RIBS AND AN EMBOSSED STITCH ARE THE MORE SUBTLE DETAILS OF THIS SMOULDERING SWEATER. DESIGNED BY BETTY BARNDEN

## MATERIALS

14 (15) × 25 g balls 3 Suisses Soiree
Pair each 2¼ mm (No 13) and 3¼ mm (No 10) knitting needles
2¾ mm (No 12) and 2¼ mm (No 13) circular knitting needles, 100 cm long
Cable needle

## MEASUREMENTS

To fit bust 81-86 (91-97) cm, 32-34 (36-38) in
Actual measurement – 96 (110) cm, 38 (43) in
Length – 68 (70) cm
Sleeve length – 43 (45) cm
Figures in brackets are for larger size

## TENSION

35 sts and 42 rows to 10 cm measured over patt of chart on 3¼ mm needles

## ABBREVIATIONS

alt – alternate; beg – beginning; c 4 b – sl next 2 sts on to cable needle and hold at back, k 2 then k 2 from cable needle; cm – centimetres; cont – continue; dec – decrease; foll – following; in – inches; inc – increase; k – knit; p – purl; patt – pattern; psso – pass slipped stitch over; rem – remain(ing); rep – repeat; sl – slip; st(s) – stitch(es); tbl – through back of loops; tog – together

## BACK

With 2¼ mm needles, cast on 164 (184) sts.
Work in cable rib patt thus:
**1st row (right side)** K 1, *k 2, p 2, k 4, p 2; rep from * to last 3 sts, k 3.
**2nd row** K 1, *p 2, k 2, p 4, k 2; rep from * to last 3 sts, p 2, k 1.

**3rd row** K 1, *k 2, p 2, c 4 b, p 2; rep from * to last 3 sts, k 3.
**4th row** As 2nd.
These 4 rows form cable rib patt.
Rep 1st to 4th rows 6 times, then work 1st to 3rd rows again.
**Inc row** Patt 14 (11), *inc in next st, patt 26 (17); rep from * 4 (8) times, inc in next st, patt 14 (10). 170 (194) sts.
Change to 3¼ mm needles.
Cont in patt from chart thus:
**1st row (right side)** K 1, reading row 1 of chart from right to left, rep the 24 sts to last st, k 1.
**2nd row** K 1, reading row 2 of chart from left to right, rep the 24 sts to last st, k 1.
Beg with row 3 of chart, cont until row 32 has been worked **.
Rep the 32 rows of chart 3 times, then work rows 1 to 18 (1 to 20) again.
A total of 146 (148) rows of patt have been worked from top of rib.
Mark each end of last row with a thread to denote start of armholes.
Work rows 19 to 32 (21 to 32).
Rep the 32 rows of chart 2 (3) times.
**1st size only:** Work rows 1 to 24.
**Both sizes:** 102 (108) rows have been worked after markers.

### Neck Shaping

**1st row (right side)** Patt 43 (55) sts, turn.
Keeping patt correct, cont on these sts only for 1st side. Leave rem sts on a spare needle.
**2nd row** P 2 tog, patt to end.
**3rd row** Patt to last 2 sts, k 2 tog.
Rep 2nd and 3rd rows twice. 37 (49) sts.
Patt 1 row, thus ending with row 32 (8).

### Shoulder Shaping

Cast off 9 (12) sts at beg of next row and on the foll 2 alt rows. Patt 1 row.
Cast off rem 10 (13) sts.
**Next row** With right side facing, sl centre 84 sts on to a spare needle, rejoin yarn to inner end of rem 43 (55) sts and patt to end.
**Next row** Patt to last 2 sts, p 2 tog tbl.
**Next row** Sl 1, k 1, psso, patt to end.
Rep last 2 rows twice. 37 (49) sts. Patt 2 rows, thus ending with row 1 (9).

### Shoulder Shaping

Work as for 1st side.

### FRONT

Work as back to **.
Rep 32 rows of chart once.

### Neck Shaping

**1st row (right side)** Patt 85 (97) sts, turn.
Keeping patt correct, cont on these sts only for 1st side.
Leave rem sts on a spare needle.
**2nd row** Patt to end.
**3rd row** Patt to last 2 sts, k 2 tog.

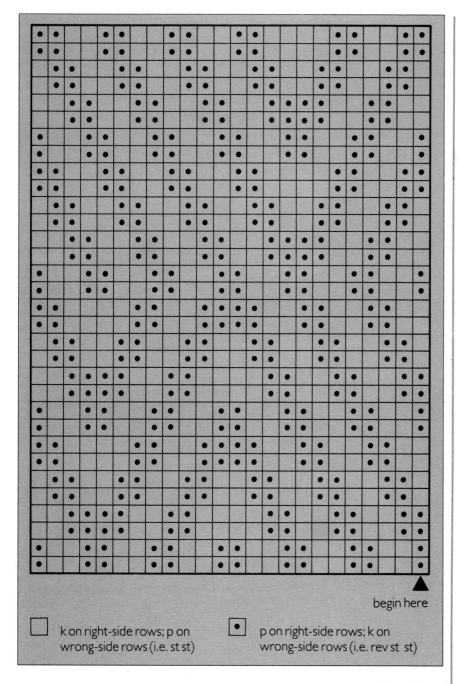

begin here

| | k on right-side rows; p on wrong-side rows (i.e. st st) | | • | p on right-side rows; k on wrong-side rows (i.e. rev st st) |

4th row until there are 128 (132) sts, working inc sts into patt.
Inc 1 st at each end of every right-side row until there are 182 (194) sts.
Patt straight until sleeve measures 47 (49) cm from cast-on edge, ending with a wrong-side row. Cast off.

## NECKBAND
Join shoulder seams.
With right side facing and using 2¾ mm circular needle, pick up and k 163 (168) sts evenly up right front neck and 12 sts down right back neck, k across 84 sts at centre back, pick up and k 12 sts up left back neck and 163 (168) sts down left front neck. 434 (444) sts.
Work forwards and back in rows.
Beg with 2nd row, work 27 rows in cable rib patt, ending with a 4th row.
Change to 2¼ mm circular needle and patt a further 28 rows. Cast off in rib.

## MAKING UP
Sew on sleeves between markers. Join side and sleeve seams, reversing seam for turn-back cuff. Overlap neckband at centre front as shown and sew row-ends to sides of neck shaping.

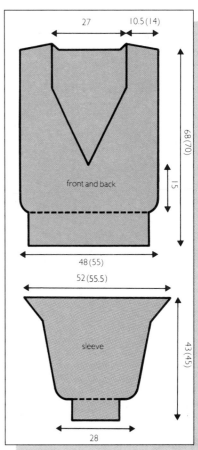

Rep last 2 rows until 61 (73) sts rem, ending with a wrong-side row.
Dec 1 st at neck edge on next row and every foll 4th row until 53 (64) sts rem, ending with a right-side row. Patt 3 (1) rows.
Mark armhole edge of last row with a contrast thread.
Cont to dec on every 4th row from previous dec until 37 (49) sts rem.
Patt straight until front matches back to shoulder, ending at side edge.

### Shoulder Shaping
Work as for back.
**Next row** With right side facing, rejoin yarn to inner end of 85 (97) sts on spare needle and patt to end.
**Next row** Patt to end.
**Next row** Sl 1, k 1, psso, patt to end.
Complete to match 1st side.

### SLEEVES
With 2¼ mm needles, cast on 84 sts.
Work 32 rows in cable rib patt as back.
**Inc row** Patt 3, *inc in next st, patt 5; rep from * 12 times, inc in next st, patt 2. 98 sts.
Change to 3¼ mm needles.
### NOTE
Wrong side of cuff is facing as row 1 of chart is worked to allow for turn back.
Cont from chart as given for back, inc 1 st at each end of 5th row and every foll

DEEP PURPLE

# DEEP PURPLE

## PERFECT PARTNERS

A SKIMPY LITTLE SINGLET AND A LUXURIOUS SMOKING JACKET BRING THE TWINSET INTO THE EXCITING EIGHTIES. DESIGNED BY BETTY BARNDEN

### MATERIALS

**Jacket**
16 (17, 17, 18) × 25 g balls Avocet Alpaca Mohair shade 105 (M)
3 × 50 g balls Avocet Soiree shade 511 (A)
Pair each 4½ mm (No 7) and 5½ mm (No 5) knitting needles
4½ mm (No 7) circular needle 100 cm long
Shoulder pads

**Singlet**
7 (8, 9, 9) × 50 g balls Avocet Soiree shade 511
Pair each 4½ mm (No 7) and 5½ mm (No 5) knitting needles

### MEASUREMENTS

**Jacket**
To fit bust 81 (86, 91, 97) cm, 32 (34, 36, 38) in
Actual measurement – 104 (109, 114, 120) cm, 41 (43, 45, 47) in
Length – 62 (64, 66, 68) cm
Sleeve length – 43 cm

**Singlet**
To fit bust 81 (86, 91, 97) cm, 32 (34, 36, 38) in
Actual measurement – 80 (85, 90, 95) cm, 31½ (33½, 35½, 37½) in
Length – 56 (57, 58, 59) cm
Figures in brackets are for larger sizes

### TENSION

**Jacket**
15 sts and 20 rows to 10 cm measured over st-st on 5½ mm needles using M

**Singlet**
24 sts and 30 rows to 10 cm measured over diagonal rib on 5½ mm needles

### ABBREVIATIONS

alt – alternate; beg – beginning; cm – centimetres; cont – continue; dec – decrease; foll – following; in – inches; inc – increase; k – knit; m 1 – make 1 st by picking up the strand between sts and k it through the back of the loop; p – purl; patt – pattern; rem – remain(ing); rep – repeat; sl – slip; st(s) – stitch(es); st-st – stocking stitch; tog – together

DEEP PURPLE

## JACKET
## BACK

With 4½ mm needles and A, cast on 80 (84, 88, 92) sts. Work 12 rows st-st. Change to 5½ mm needles and M. Fold work in half with cast-on edge behind sts on needle.
**Next row (close hem)** *K next st from needle tog with corresponding st from cast-on edge; rep from * to end. ** Beg with a p row, work in st-st. Cont straight until back measures 40 (41, 42, 43) cm, ending with a p row.

### Armhole Shaping

Cast off 6 sts at beg of next 2 rows. Dec 1 st at each end of every right-side row until 56 (60, 64, 68) sts rem. Cont straight until work measures 62 (64, 66, 68) cm, ending with a p row.

### Shoulder Shaping

Cast off 6 (6, 6, 7) sts at beg of next 4 rows, then cast off 5 (6, 7, 6) sts at beg of next 2 rows.
Cast off rem 22 (24, 26, 28) sts.

### POCKET LININGS

**Make 2** With 5½ mm needles and M, cast on 26 sts.
Work in st-st for 28 rows. Break yarn and leave sts on a stitch holder.

### LEFT FRONT

With 4½ mm needles and A, cast on 40 (42, 44, 46) sts. Work as back to **
Beg with a p row, work 29 rows st-st. ***

**Pocket Opening row** K 8 (10, 12, 14) sts, sl next 26 sts on to a stitch holder, k across sts of one pocket lining, k 6.
P 1 row.

### Front Shaping

**1st row** K to last st, m 1, k 1.
Cont to inc at front edge thus on every foll 6th row until front matches back to armhole, ending with a p row.

### Armhole Shaping

Cast off 6 sts at beg of next row, then dec 1 st at armhole edge on next 6 right-side rows, AT THE SAME TIME inc at front edge as before.
Keeping armhole edge straight, cont to inc at front edge until there are 43 (45, 47, 49) sts.
Work straight until front matches back to shoulder, ending with a p row.

### Shoulder Shaping

Cast off 6 (6, 6, 7) sts at beg of next row and on the foll alt row.
P 1 row. Cast off 5 (6, 7, 6) sts at beg of next row.
Work 13 (15, 17, 19) rows staight on rem 26 (27, 28, 29) sts. Cast off.

### RIGHT FRONT

Work as left front to ***
**Pocket Opening row** K 6, sl next 26 sts on to a stitch holder, k across sts of 2nd pocket lining, k 8 (10, 12, 14).  P 1 row.

### Front Shaping

**1st row** K 1, m 1, k to end.

Complete to match left front, working 1 extra row before armhole shaping and shoulder shaping.

### SLEEVES

With 4½ mm needles and A, cast on 50 (52, 54, 56) sts.
Work as back to **
Beg with a p row, work in st-st.
Inc 1 st at each end of every 10th (10th, 8th, 8th) row until there are 64 (68, 72, 76) sts.
Cont straight until sleeve measures 43 cm, ending with a p row.

### Top Shaping

Cast off 6 sts at beg of next 2 rows.
Dec 1 st at each end of every right-side row until 32 (36, 40, 44) sts rem, ending with a p row.
Dec 1 st at each end of every row until 24 sts rem. Cast off.

### POCKET TOPS

With right side facing, using 4½ mm needles and A, k across 26 sts on stitch holder. Beg p, work 11 rows st-st. Cast off.

### RIGHT FRONT BAND

With right side facing, using 4½ mm circular needle and A, pick up and k 4 sts from edge of lower hem, pick up and k evenly 139 (144, 148, 153) sts along rem front edge and collar extension. 143 (148, 152, 157) sts.
Beg p, work 11 rows st-st.. Cast off or leave sts on spare yarn (see making up).

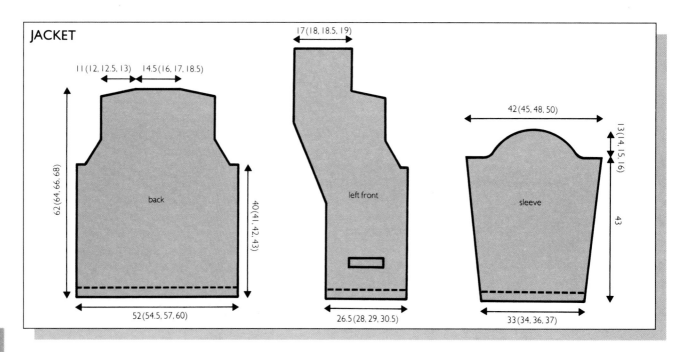

JACKET

back — 11 (12, 12.5, 13)  14.5 (16, 17, 18.5) — 62 (64, 66, 68) — 40 (41, 42, 43) — 52 (54.5, 57, 60)

left front — 17 (18, 18.5, 19) — 26.5 (28, 29, 30.5)

sleeve — 42 (45, 48, 50) — 13 (14, 15, 16) — 43 — 33 (34, 36, 37)

## LEFT FRONT BAND
Work to match right front band.

## MAKING UP
Press lightly, omitting edgings. Join shoulder seams. Join cast-off edges of collar extensions and row ends of bands with seam to inside of folded collar. Centring this seam at back neck, sew down collar. Fold and hem front bands, either oversewing carefully a cast-off edge (remembering that this will be the right side on collar), or back stitching sts left on spare yarn taking care to match each st loop with a picked-up st. Hem pocket tops. Set in sleeves. Join side and sleeve seams.

## SINGLET
### BACK
With 4½ mm needles, cast on 98 (104, 110, 116) sts.
**1st rib row (right side)** K 1, *p 3, k 3; rep from * to last st, k 1.
**2nd row** P 1, * p 3, k 3; rep from * to last st, p 1.
Rep these 2 rows 7 times.
Change to 5½ mm needles.
Cont in patt thus:
**1st row (right side)** K 4, *p 3, k 3; rep from * to last 4 sts, p 3, k 1.
**2nd row** P 1, *k 3, p 3; rep from * to last st, p 1.
**3rd row** *K 3, p 3; rep from * to last 2 sts, k 2.
**4th row** P 2, *k 3, p 3; rep from * to end.
**5th row** K 2, *p 3, k 3; rep from * to end.
**6th row** *P 3, k 3; rep from * to last 2 sts, p 2.
**7th row** K 1, *p 3, k 3; rep from * to last st, k 1.
**8th row** P 4, *k 3, p 3; rep from * to last 4 sts, k 3, p 1.
**9th row** K 1, p 2, *k 3, p 3; rep from * to last 5 sts, k 3, p 1, k 1.
**10th row** P 1, k 1, *p 3, k 3; rep from * to last 6 sts, p 3, k 2, p 1.
**11th row** K 1, p 1, *k 3, p 3; rep from * to last 6 sts, k 3, p 2, k 1.
**12th row** P 1, k 2, *p 3, k 3; rep from * to last 5 sts, p 3, k 1, p 1.
These 12 rows form patt.
Rep patt 7 times. 96 rows.

### Armhole Shaping
Keeping patt correct, cast off 12 sts at beg of next 2 rows.
Dec 1 st at each end of next 12 (14, 14, 16) rows, then on the foll 3 (4, 4, 5) alt rows. 44 (44, 50, 50) sts. **
Patt 12 rows without shaping.

### Neck Shaping
**1st row** Patt 16 sts, turn.
Cont on these sts only for 1st side and leave rem sts on a spare needle.
Cast off 3 sts at beg of next row.
Dec 1 st at neck edge on next 5 rows, then on the foll 2 alt rows. 6 sts.
Patt straight for 16 (14, 16, 14) rows. Cast off.
**Next row** With right side facing, sl centre 12 (12, 18, 18) sts on to a stitch holder, rejoin yarn to inner end of rem 16 sts and patt to end.
Complete to match 1st side.

### FRONT
Work as back to **.
Complete as back from neck shaping but patt 12 extra rows straight before casting off.

### NECK EDGING
Join left shoulder strap.
With right side facing and using 4½ mm needles, pick up and k 22 sts evenly down right back neck, k 12 (12, 18, 18) sts across centre back, pick up and k 22 sts up left back neck, pick up and k 30 sts down left front neck, k 12 (12, 18, 18) sts across centre, pick up and k 30 sts up right front neck. 128 (128, 140, 140) sts. K 1 row. Cast off.

### ARMHOLE EDGINGS
Join right shoulder strap.
With right side facing and using 4½ mm needles, pick up and k 116 (120, 124, 130) sts evenly around armhole. K 1 row. Cast off.

### MAKING UP
Join side seams.

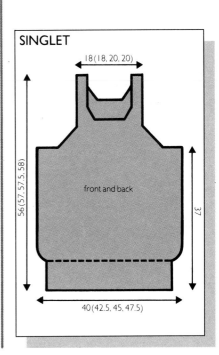

SINGLET

18 (18, 20, 20)

56 (57, 57.5, 58)

37

front and back

40 (42.5, 45, 47.5)

INDIAN SUMMER

# INDIAN SUMMER

## DELHI

**A**N ESSENTIALLY FEMININE CRICKET SWEATER COMBINES A SOPHISTICATED YARN AND SOFTLY WRAPPED CABLES. DESIGNED BY PAT QUIROGA

### MATERIALS
8 (9, 10) × 50 g balls Tootal Avalon
Pair each 4½ mm (No 7) and 5½ mm (No 5) knitting needles
Cable needle
Shoulder pads

### MEASUREMENTS
To fit bust 86 (91, 97) cm, 34 (36, 38) in
Actual measurement – 108 (113, 118) cm, 42.5 (44.5, 46.5) in
Length – 70 cm
Sleeve length – 44 cm
Figures in round brackets are for larger sizes

### TENSION
16 sts and 20 rows to 10 cm over st-st on 5½ mm needles

### ABBREVIATIONS
beg – beginning; c 15 b – sl next 7 sts on to cable needle and leave at back of work, k 8 then k 7 from cable needle; c 15 f – sl next 8 sts on to cable needle and leave at front of work, k 7 then k 8 from cable needle; cm – centimetres; cont – continue; dec – decrease; foll – following; in – inches; inc – increase; k – knit; m 1 – make 1 st by picking up the strand between sts and k it through the back of the loop; p – purl; patt – pattern; psso – pass slipped stitch over; rem – remain(ing); rep – repeat; sl – slip; st(s) – stitch(es); st-st – stocking

stitch; tog – together; yb – yarn back; yfwd – yarn forward
Work instructions in square brackets the number of times given

## BACK

With 4½ mm needles, cast on 76 (76, 84) sts.
**1st rib row (right side)** K 1, *k 2, p 2; rep from * to last 3 sts, k 3.
**2nd rib row** K 1, *p 2, k 2; rep from * to last 3 sts, p 2, k 1.
Rep 1st and 2nd rib rows 16 times, then work 1st rib row again.
**Next row** Rib 2, [m 1, rib 4] 5 (7, 5) times, m 1, rib 32 (16, 40), [m 1, rib 4] 5 (7, 5) times, m 1, rib 2.
88 (92, 96) sts.
Change to 5½ mm needles.

Cont in st-st. Work 76 (74, 72) rows.

### Armhole Shaping

Cast off 6 (7, 8) sts at beg of next 2 rows.
Dec 1 st at each end of the next 8 rows. 60 (62, 64) sts.
Work 22 (24, 26) rows straight.

### Neck Shaping

**1st row** K 11 (12, 13), cast off next 38 sts, k to end.
Cont on last 11 (12, 13) sts only for 1st side.
Dec 1 st at neck edge on the next 5 rows.
Cast off rem 6 (7, 8) sts.
With wrong side facing, rejoin yarn to inner end of rem 11 (12, 13) sts and

complete to match 1st side.

## FRONT

With 4½ mm needles, cast on 86 (86, 94) sts.
**1st row (right side)** K 1, [k 2, p 2] 6 (6, 7) times, *k 4, [yfwd, sl 1, yb, k 1] 3 times, yfwd, sl 1, yb, k 4*, p 2, k 2, p 2, **k 4, [sl 1, k 1] 3 times, sl 1, k 4**, [p 2, k 2] 6 (6, 7) times, k 1.
**2nd row** K 1, [p 2, k 2] 6 (6, 7) times, **p 5, [yb, sl 1, yfwd, p 1] 3 times, p 4**, k 2, p 2, k 2, *p 5, [sl 1, p 1] 3 times, p 4*, [k 2, p 2] 6 (6, 7) times, k 1.
**3rd row** Rib 25 (25, 29), *k 4 [sl next st on to cable needle and leave at back of work, k 1] 3 times, k the 3 sts from cable needle, k 5*, p 2, k 2, p 2, **k 4, [sl next st on to cable needle and leave at front of work, k 1] 3 times, k 3 from cable needle, k 5**, rib 25 (25, 29).
**4th row** Rib 25 (25, 29), p 15, k 2, p 2, k 2, p 15, rib 25 (25, 29).
Now beg cable patt over centre 40 sts thus:
**1st row** Rib 23 (23, 27), p 2, k 15, p 2, k 2, p 2, k 15, p 2, rib 23 (23, 27).
**2nd row** Rib 23 (23, 27), k 2, p 15, k 2, p 2, k 2, p 15, k 2, rib 23 (23, 27).
**3rd to 12 rows** Rep 1st and 2nd rows 5 times.
**13th row** Rib 23 (23, 27), p 2, c 15 b, p 2, k 2, p 2, c 15 f, p 2, rib 23 (23, 27).
**14th row** As 2nd.
**15th to 20th rows** Work 1st and 2nd rows 3 times.
These 20 rows set cable patt over centre 40 sts.
Rep 1st to 11th rows.
**Next row** [Rib 2, m 1] 7 (11, 5) times, [rib 4, m 1] 2 (0, 4) times, p 1, work 12th row of cable patt over next 40 sts, p 1, [m 1, rib 4] 2 (0, 4) times, [m 1, rib 2] 7 (11, 5) times.
104 (108, 112) sts.
Change to 5½ mm needles.
Cont in cable patt over centre 40 sts but change to st-st over 32 (34, 36) sts at each side.
Work 66 (64, 62) rows.

### Neck Shaping

**1st row** K 30 (32, 34), k 2 tog, patt 20 sts, turn.
Cont on these sts only for 1st side.
Keeping patt correct, patt 3 rows.
**Dec row** K to last 22 sts, k 2 tog, patt 20.
Patt 3 rows.
Rep dec row.
Patt 1 row. 49 (51, 53) sts.

### ***Armhole Shaping

Cont to dec at neck on every 4th row from previous dec as before, AND AT THE SAME TIME, cast off 6 (7, 8) sts at beg of next row.

Patt 1 row – omit this row on 2nd side.

Dec 1 st at armhole edge on the next 8 rows.

Cont to dec at neck only until 26 (27, 28) sts rem ***.

Patt 3 (5, 7) rows straight, thus ending at armhole edge.

### Shoulder Shaping

**Next row** Cast off 5 (6, 7) sts, patt to end. 21 sts.

**Next row** K 3, p 7, yb, sl 1, yfwd, turn.

**Next row** Sl 1, k 7, p 2, k 1.

**Next row** K 3, p 15, k 3.

### Back Extension

**1st row (right side)** K 1, p 2, k 15, p 2, k 1.

**2nd row** K 3, p 15, k 3.

**3rd row** K 1, p 2, k 9, yfwd, sl 1, yb, turn.

**4th row** Sl 1, p 9, k 3.

**5th row** K 1, p 2, k 4, yfwd, sl 1, yb, turn.

**6th row** Sl 1, p 4, k 3.

**7th to 14th rows** Rep 1st to 6th rows once, then work 1st and 2nd rows again.

**15th row** K 1, p 2, c 15 b, p 2, k 1.

**16th row** As 2nd.

**17th to 30th rows** Rep 1st to 6th rows twice, then work 1st and 2nd rows again.

Cast off. Mark last cast-off st with a coloured thread.

With right side facing rejoin yarn to inner end of rem 52 (54, 56) sts.

**Dec row** Patt 20, sl 1, k 1, psso, k to end.

Patt 3 rows.

Rep last 4 rows once.

Rep dec row. Patt 2 rows. 49 (51, 53) sts. Work to match 1st side from *** to ***.

Patt 4 (6, 8) rows straight, thus ending at armhole edge.

### Shoulder Shaping

**Next row** Cast off 5 (6, 7) sts, patt to end. 21 sts.

**Next row** K 1, p 2, k 7, yfwd, sl 1, yb, turn.

**Next row** Sl 1, p 7, k 3.

### Back Extension

**1st row** K 1, p 2, k 15, p 2, k 1.

**2nd row** K 3, p 9, yb, sl 1, yfwd, turn.

**3rd row** Sl 1, k 9, p 2, k 1.

**4th row** K 3, p 4, yb, sl 1, yfwd, turn.

**5th row** Sl 1, k 4, p 2, k 1.

**6th row** K 3, p 15, k 3.

**7th to 12th rows** As 1st to 6th rows.

**13th row** As 1st.

**14th row** As 6th.

**15th row** K 1, p 2, c 15 f, p 2, k 1.

**16th row** As 6th.

**17th to 28th rows** Rep 1st to 6th rows twice.

**29th row** As 1st.

**30th row** As 6th.

Cast off.

### RIGHT SLEEVE

With 4½ mm needles, cast on 41 sts.

**1st row (right side)** K 1, [k 2, p 2] 3 times, work from * to * of 1st row of front welt, [p 2, k 2] 3 times, k 1.

**2nd row** K 1, [p 2, k 2] 3 times, work from * to * of 2nd row of front welt, [k 2, p 2] 3 times, k 1.

**3rd row** Rib 13, work from * to * of 3rd row of front welt, rib 13.

**4th row** Rib 13, p 15, rib 13.

Now beg cable patt over centre 19 sts thus:

**1st row** Rib 11, p 2, k 15, p 2, rib 11.

**2nd row** Rib 11, k 2, p 15, k 2, rib 11.

**3rd to 12th rows** Rep 1st and 2nd rows 5 times.

**13th row** Rib 11, p 2, c 15 b, p 2, rib 11.

**14th row** As 2nd.

**15th row** As 1st.

**16th row** [Rib 2, m 1] 5 times, p 1, k 2, p 15, k 2, p 1, [m 1, rib 2] 5 times. 51 sts.

Change to 5½ mm needles.

**17th row** K 16, p 2, k 15, p 2, k 16.

**18th row** P 16, k 2, p 15, k 2, p 16.

**19th and 20th rows** As 17th and 18th rows.

These 20 rows set cable patt over centre 19 sts.

Cont in cable patt over centre 19 sts working in st-st over rem sts.

Inc 1 st at each end of next row and every foll 4th row until there are 71 (73, 75) sts.

Patt 31 (27, 23) rows straight.

### Top Shaping

Keeping patt correct, cast off 6 (7, 8) sts at beg of next 2 rows.

Dec 1 st at each end of next 8 rows. 43 sts.

Work 20 (22, 24) rows straight.

**Next row** [K 3 tog] 4 times, p 2 tog, [k 3 tog] 3 times, [sl 1, k 2 tog, psso] twice, p 2 tog, [sl 1, k 2 tog, psso] 4 times. 15 sts.

**Next row** P.

**Next row** [K 2 tog] 3 times, k 3, [sl 1, k 1, psso] 3 times.

**Next row** P.

Cast off rem 9 sts.

### LEFT SLEEVE

Work as right sleeve but on 1st to 3rd rows of cuff work from ** to ** of front welt not from * to *. Work c 15 f instead of c 15 b.

### NECK EDGING

With right side facing, using 4½ mm needles and beg at marker on left back extension, pick up and k 60 (62, 64) sts evenly to centre of 'V' and 60 (62, 64) sts evenly to cast-off edge of right back extension. Cast off knitwise.

### MAKING UP

Join shoulder seams. Join cast-off edges of back extensions, then with seam to centre back neck, sew in place. Join side and sleeve seams. Set in sleeves. Sew in shoulder pads. Press seams.

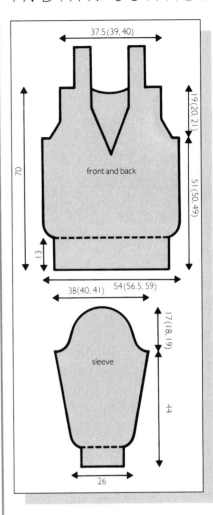

# MADRAS

A TOWELLING-TEXTURED SPORTS SHIRT HAS PADDED SHOULDERS AND A DEEP CABLED WELT. DESIGNED BY LESLEY STANFIELD

## MATERIALS

11 (12, 12, 13) 50 g balls Copley Sandpiper
Pair each 3¼ mm (No 10) and 3¾ mm (No 9) knitting needles
Set of four 3¼ mm (No 10) double-pointed needles
Cable needle
Shoulder pads

## MEASUREMENTS

To fit bust 81 (86, 91, 97) cm, 32 (34, 36, 38) in
Actual measurement – 96 (102, 108, 114) cm, 38 (40, 42½, 45) in
Length – 64 (65, 66, 67) cm
Sleeve length – 43 cm
Figures in brackets are for larger sizes

## TENSION

20 sts and 28 rows to 10 cm over st-st on 3¾ mm needles

## ABBREVIATIONS

alt – alternate; beg – beginning; c 4 – sl next 2 sts on to cable needle and hold at front, k 2 then k 2 from cable needle; cm – centimetres; cont – continue; dec – decrease; foll – following; g-st – garter st; in – inches; inc – increase; k – knit; m 1 – make 1 st by picking up the strand between sts and k it through the back of the loop; p – purl; rem – remain(ing); rep – repeat; sl – slip; st(s) – stitch(es); st-st – stocking stitch; tog – together
Work instructions in square brackets the number of times given

## BACK

With pair of 3¼ mm needles, cast on 77 (82, 87, 92) sts.
**1st row (right side)** P 2, *k 3, p 2; rep from * to end.
**2nd row** K 2, *p 3, k 2; rep from * to end.

# INDIAN SUMMER

**3rd row** As 1st.

**4th row** K 2, *p twice into next st, p 2, k 2; rep from * to end. 92 (98, 104, 110) sts.

**5th row** P 2, *c 4, p 2; rep from * to end.

**6th row** K 2, *p 4, k 2; rep from * to end.

**7th row** P 2, *k 4, p 2; rep from * to end.

**8th row** As 6th.

**9th row** As 7th.

**10th row** As 6th.

Rep 5th to 10th rows 4 times, then work 5th to 7th rows again.

Change to 3¾ mm needles.

**Next row (wrong side)** P.

Cont in st-st, inc 1 st at each end of every 20th row until there are 98 (104, 110, 116) sts.

Cont straight until work measures 40 cm ending with a wrong-side row.

## Armhole shaping

Dec 1 st at each end of every row until 70 (76, 82, 88) sts rem.*

Cont straight until work measures 64 (65, 66, 67) cm ending with a wrong-side row. Leave sts on a spare needle.

## FRONT

Work as back to *.

Cont straight until work measures 58 (59, 60, 61) cm, ending with a wrong-side row.

## Neck Shaping

**1st row** K 31 (33, 35, 37) sts, turn.

Cont on these sts only for 1st side.

Leave rem sts on a spare needle.

Dec 1 st at neck edge on the next 8 rows. 23 (25, 27, 29) sts.

Cont straight until front matches back to shoulder. Leave sts on a holder.

**Next row** With right side facing, sl centre 8 (10, 12, 14) sts on to a stitch holder, rejoin yarn to inner end of rem 31 (33, 35, 37) sts and k to end.

Complete to match 1st side.

## SLEEVES

With pair of 3¼ mm needles, cast on 38 (42, 46, 50) sts.

Work 6 rows g-st.

Change to 3¾ mm needles.

Cont in st-st, inc 1 st at each end of 1st and every foll 4th row until there are 90 (94, 98, 102) sts, ending with a wrong-side row.

Inc 1 st at each end of next and alt rows until there are 104 (108, 112, 116) sts, ending with a wrong-side row.

## Top Shaping

Dec 1 st at each end of every row until 76 (80, 84, 88) sts rem. Cast off loosely.

## COLLAR

Join right shoulder seam thus: place wrong sides tog. With back facing and using 3¾ mm needles, cast off first 23 (25, 27, 29) sts from back and all right front shoulder sts tog knitwise, taking 1 st from each needle tog each time. Sl 24 (26, 28, 30) sts from centre back on to a stitch holder. Join left shoulder as for right shoulder.

Mark centre of front neck with a contrast thread.

With right side facing and 3¼ mm double pointed needles, k 4 (5, 6, 7) sts from side of centre front marker, pick up and k evenly 16 sts up right front neck, k across 24 (26, 28, 30) sts of back neck, pick up and k 16 sts down left front neck, k 4 (5, 6, 7) sts from other side of centre front marker. 64 (68, 72, 76) sts.

Working forwards and back in rows, work 8 rows g-st.

**Next row** K 4 (5, 6, 7), [m 1, k 3] 4 times, [m 1, k 2] 4 times, m 1, k 16 (18, 20, 22), [m 1, k 2] 4 times, [m 1, k 3] 4 times, m 1, k 4 (5, 6, 7). 82 (86, 90, 94) sts.

Work 14 rows g-st. Cast off loosely.

## MAKING UP

Press, omitting cables and g-st. Set in sleeves. Join side and sleeve seams. Sew in shoulder pads.

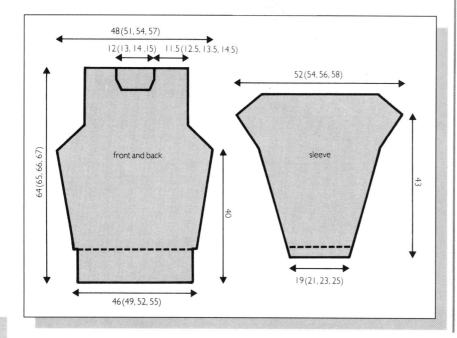

front and back

48 (51, 54, 57)

12 (13, 14, 15)   11.5 (12.5, 13.5, 14.5)

64 (65, 66, 67)

40

46 (49, 52, 55)

sleeve

52 (54, 56, 58)

43

19 (21, 23, 25)

# JAIPUR

*A WIDE, WIDE T-SHIRT IN CHALKY COTTON IS PUNCTUATED BY CLUSTERS OF SMALL CABLES. DESIGNED BY DEBBIE BLISS*

## MATERIALS

16 × 50 g balls Hayfield Raw Cotton
Pair each 3 mm (No 11), 3 1/4 mm (No 10) and 4 mm (No 8) knitting needles
Cable needle

## MEASUREMENTS

One size, to fit up to bust 102 cm, 40 in
Actual measurement – 136 cm, 53 1/2 in
Length – 56 cm
Sleeve length – 43 cm

## TENSION

25 sts and 28 rows to 10 cm over patt on 4 mm needles

## ABBREVIATIONS

alt – alternate; beg – beginning; c 6 – slip next 3 sts on to cable needle and hold at front, k 3 then k 3 from cable needle; cm – centimetres; cont – continue; dec –decrease; in – inches; inc – increase; k – knit; m 1 – make 1 st by picking up the strand between sts and k it through the back of the loop; p – purl; patt – pattern; rem – remain; rep – repeat; sl – slip; st(s) – stitch(es)

## BACK

With 3 mm needles, cast on 147 sts.
**1st row (right side)** K 1, *p 1, k 1; rep from * to end.
**2nd row** P 1, *k 1, p 1; rep from * to end.
Rep these 2 rows for 4 cm, ending with a right-side row.
**Inc row** Rib 2, *m 1, rib 6; rep from * to last st, m 1, rib 1. 172 sts.
Change to 4 mm needles.
Cont in patt thus:
**1st row (right side)** K 11, *p 6, k 18; rep from * to last 17 sts, p 6, k 11.
**2nd and alt rows** P 11, *k 6, p 18; rep from * to last 17 sts, k 6, p 11.
**3rd row** K 11, *p 6, c 6, k 12; rep from

* to last 17 sts, p 6, c 6, k 5.
**5th, 7th and 9th rows** As 1st row.
**11th row** As 3rd row.
**13th, 15th and 17th rows** As 1st row.
**19th row** As 3rd row.
**21st row** As 1st row.
**23rd row** K 5, c 6, *p 6, k 12, c 6; rep from * to last 17 sts, p 6, k 11.
**25th, 27th and 29th rows** As 1st row.
**31st row** As 23rd row.
**33rd, 35th and 37th rows** As 1st row.
**39th row** As 23rd row.
**40th row** As 2nd row.
These 40 rows form patt.**
Patt straight until back measures 51 cm, ending with a wrong-side row.

### Neck Shaping

**1st row** Patt 68 sts, turn.
Keeping patt correct, cont on these sts only for 1st side and leave rem sts on a spare needle.
***Cast off 5 sts at beg of next row, 4 sts on the next alt row, 3 sts on the next alt row, 2 sts on the next alt row and 1 st on the next alt row. 53 sts.
Work 6 rows straight.

### Shoulder Shaping

Cast off 27 sts at beg of next row. Patt 1 row. Cast off rem 26 sts.
**Next row** With right side facing, sl centre 36 sts on to a stitch holder, rejoin yarn to inner end of rem 68 sts.
Complete to match 1st side from ***.

## FRONT

Work as back to **.
Patt straight until front measures 22 row less than back to shoulder, ending with a wrong-side row.

### Neck Shaping

**1st row** Patt 68 sts, turn.
Keeping patt correct, cont on these sts only for 1st side and leave rem sts on a

spare needle.
****Cast off 4 sts at beg of next row, 3 sts on the next alt row, 2 sts on the next alt row. Dec 1 st at beg of foll 6 alt rows. Work 4 rows straight.

### Shoulder Shaping

Work as back.
**Next row** As back.
Complete to match 1st side from ****.

## SLEEVES

With 3 mm needles, cast on 63 sts.
Rib as back for 5 cm, ending with a right-side row.
**Inc row** Rib 2, *m 1, rib 5; rep from * to last st, m 1, rib 1. 76 sts.
Change to 4 mm needles.
Cont in patt thus:
**1st row** K 11, *p 6, k 18; rep from * to last 17 sts, p 6, k 11.
**2nd row** P 11, *k 6, p 18; rep from * to last 17 sts, k 6, p 11.
Cont in patt as set, inc 1 st at each end of next and foll alt rows and working inc sts into patt, until there are 180 sts.
Patt 1 row. Cast off.

## NECKBAND

Join right shoulder seam.
With right side facing, using 3 1/4 mm needles pick up and k 22 sts evenly down left front neck, k across 36 sts at centre front, pick up and k 22 sts up right front neck, pick up and k 14 sts down right back neck, k across 36 sts of centre back neck, pick up and k 14 sts up left back neck. 144 sts.
Work 3 cm in k 1, p 1 rib. Cast off.

## MAKING UP

Join left shoulder and neckband seam. Sew on sleeves. Join side and sleeve seams. Press seams.

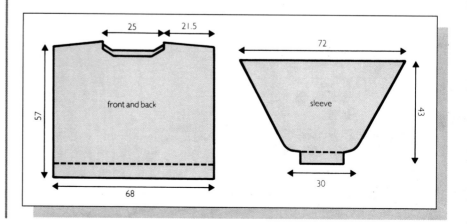

FIFTIES FOREVER

BE-BOP

# FIFTIES FOREVER

SILVER BEADS BLEND FIFTIES NOSTALGIA AND THE COWBOY CRAZE. THEY'RE SEWN ON TO A DECEPTIVELY DEMURE LITTLE CARDIGAN IN FINE WOOL. DESIGNED BY LESLEY STANFIELD

## MATERIALS

8 (8, 9, 9) × 50 g balls King Cole Superwash 4 ply
Pair each 2¼ mm (No 13) and 3 mm (No 11) knitting needles
Sewing thread to match yarn
Beads: 10 × P10 (large round beads used as buttons), 200 × No 4 (small round beads), 210 × PO3 (oval beads), 12 g × M13-2 (bugle beads).
Amounts are minimum quantities, except No 4 and PO3, all available from Ells & Farrier (see page 109)

## MEASUREMENTS

To fit bust 81 (86, 91, 97) cm, 32 (34, 36, 38) in
Actual measurement – 85 (90, 95, 100) cm, 33½ (35½, 37½, 39½) in
Length – 53 (54, 57, 58) cm
Sleeve length – 46 cm
Figures in round brackets are for larger sizes

## TENSION

32 sts and 40 rows to 10 cm over st-st on 3 mm needles

## ABBREVIATIONS

alt – alternate; beg – beginning; cm – centimetres; cont – continue; dec – decrease; foll – following; in – inches; inc – increase; k – knit; p – purl; rem – remain(ing); rep – repeat; sl – slip; st(s) – stitch(es); st-st – stocking stitch; tog – together
Work instructions in square brackets the number of times given

## BACK

With 2¼ mm needles, cast on 138 (146, 154, 162) sts.
Work 48 rows in k 2, p 2 rib, beg

wrong-side rows p 2.
Change to 3 mm needles and st-st.
Work 96 (96, 104, 104) rows.

## Armhole Shaping

Cast off 8 sts at beg of next 2 rows.
Dec 1 st at each end of next row and every foll alt row until 110 (114, 118, 122) sts rem, thus ending with a k row.
Work 63 rows straight, thus ending with a p row.

## Shoulder Shaping

Cast off 8 (9, 10, 11) sts at beg of next 2 rows and 9 sts on the foll 6 rows.
Leave rem 40 (42, 44, 46) sts on a stitch holder.

## RIGHT FRONT

With 2¼ mm needles, cast on 79 (83, 87, 91) sts.
Work welt thus:
**1st row** K 7, sl 1, k 7, [p 2, k 2] to end.
**2nd row** [P 2, k 2] 16 (17, 18, 19) times, p 15.
Rep 1st and 2nd rows twice.
**7th row (make buttonhole)** K 2, cast off 3 sts, k 2 including st rem on needle after casting off, sl 1, k 2, cast off 3 sts, k 2 including st rem on needle after casting off, [p 2, k 2] to end.
**8th row** [P 2, k 2] 16 (17, 18, 19) times, p 2, cast on 3 sts, p 5, cast on 3 sts, p 2.
*Rep 1st and 2nd rows 9 times.
**27th row** As 7th.
**28th row** As 8th.
Rep from * once. (A total of 48 rows have been worked).
Change to 3 mm needles.
**Work main part thus:
1st row** K 7, sl 1, k to end.
**2nd row** P.
Rep 1st and 2nd rows 9 (9, 10, 10) times.
**21st (21st, 23rd, 23rd) row** K 2, cast off 3 sts, k 2 including st rem on needle after casting off, sl 1, k 2, cast off 3 sts, k to end.
**22nd (22nd, 24th, 24th) row** P 66 (70, 74, 78), cast on 3 sts, p 5, cast on 3 sts, p 2.
Rep rows 1 to 22 (22, 24, 24) until a total of 97 (97, 105, 105) rows have been completed from **.

## Armhole Shaping

Cont to work buttonholes with 20 (20, 22, 22) rows between, AND AT THE SAME TIME, cast off 8 sts at beg of next row, then dec 1 st at armhole edge on the next 6 (8, 10, 12) right-

side rows. 65 (67, 69, 71) sts.
Cont straight, working buttonholes as before, until the 16th (16th, 18th, 18th) row after the 9th buttonhole has been worked, thus ending with a p row.

## Neck Shaping

**Next row** Sl 20 (21, 22, 23) sts on to a stitch holder, k 45 (46, 47, 48) sts.
Dec 1 st at neck edge on the next 10 rows. 35 (36, 37, 38) sts.
Work 14 (18, 16, 20) rows straight, thus ending with a k row.

## Shoulder Shaping

Cast off 8 (9, 10, 11) sts at beg of next row and 9 sts on the foll 2 alt rows.
Work 1 row. Cast off rem 9 sts.

## LEFT FRONT

With 2¼ mm needles, cast on 79 (83, 87, 91) sts.
Work welt thus:
**1st row** [K 2, p 2] 16 (17, 18, 19) times, k 7, sl 1, k 7.
**2nd row** P 15, [k 2, p 2] to end.
Rep 1st and 2nd rows 23 times.
Change to 3 mm needles.
Complete to match right front from **, omitting buttonholes.

## SLEEVES

With 2¼ mm needles, cast on 70 (74, 78, 82) sts.
Rib 8 cm as given at beg of back.
Change to 3 mm needles and cont in st-st.
Inc 1 st at each end of 1st row and every foll 8th (8th, 8th, 6th) row until there are 98 (106, 114, 122) sts.
Cont straight until sleeve measures 46 cm from cast-on edge, ending with a p row.

## Top Shaping

Cast off 8 sts at beg of next 2 rows.
Dec 1 st at each end of every row until 66 (74, 82, 90) sts rem, then at each end of every 3rd row until 34 (40, 46, 52) sts rem.
Cast off 2 sts at beg of next 4 rows. 26 (32, 38, 44) sts.
Working k 2 (0, 2, 0), [k 2 tog, k 2] to end, cast off.

## NECKBAND

Join shoulder seams.
With right side facing and using 2¼ mm needles, across sts of right front stitch holder work k 7, sl 1, k 12 (13, 14, 15), pick up and k 24 (28, 26, 30) sts

up right front neck, k across 40 (42, 44, 46) sts of back neck, pick up and k 24 (28, 26, 30) sts down left front neck, then across sts on stitch holder work k 12 (13, 14, 15), sl 1, k 7. 128 (140, 140, 152) sts.

**1st row** P 15, k 2, [p 2, k 2] to last 15 sts, p 15.

**2nd row** K 7, sl 1, k 7, p 2, [k 2, p 2] to last 15 sts, k 7, sl 1, k 7.

**3rd row** As 1st.

**4th row (buttonhole row)** K 2, cast off 3 sts, k 2 including st rem on needle after casting off, sl 1, k 2, cast off 3 sts, k 2 including st rem on needle after casting off, rib to last 15 sts, k 7, sl 1, k 7.

**5th row** P 15, rib to last 15 sts, p 2, cast on 3 sts, p 5, cast on 3 sts, p 2.

**6th row** As 2nd.

**7th row** As 1st.

Rep 6th and 7th rows once. Cast off with sts as set.

## MAKING UP

Press. Sew on beads as diagram, using knitting yarn for all except bugle beads. Start with larger flower centres and work outwards. Match left front by using rows and sts as a guide to placing motifs. To make stems, thread bugle beads with sewing thread, lay on knitting, then couch down (ie take a small st over the sewing thread between each bead). Cont the random small beads at neck around back neck. Turn in front facings and catch down, then neaten ends. Neaten buttonholes. Set in sleeves easing in fullness at top. Join side and sleeve seams. Sew on size P 10 beads as buttons.

**PATTERN FOR BEADWORK**

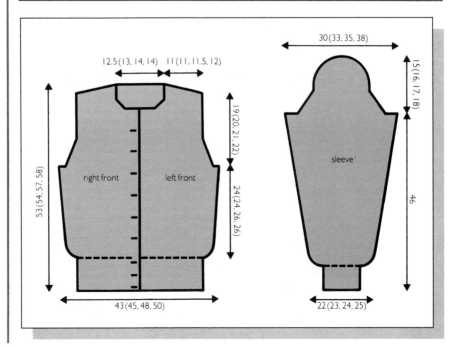

FIFTIES FOREVER

CLASSIC COLLECTION

# CLASSIC COLLECTION

## MARLBOROUGH

MORE LIKE A VAST, WARM COAT, THIS OVER-SIZED CARDIGAN HAS KNOTTED CABLES, DEEP RIBBED WELTS AND SIDE VENTS. DESIGNED BY SUZANNE RUSSELL

### MATERIALS
18 × 50 g balls Yarnworks Merino
Pair each 3¾ mm (No 9) and 4½ mm (No 7) knitting needles
Cable needle
5 buttons

### MEASUREMENTS
One size, to fit up to bust 107 cm, 42 in
Actual measurement – 153 cm, 60 in
Length – 73 cm
Sleeve length – 44 cm

### TENSION
24 sts and 26 rows to 10 cm over patt on 4½ mm needles

### ABBREVIATIONS
beg – beginning; c 4 f – sl next 3 sts on to cable needle and hold at front, p 1 then k 3 from cable needle; c 5 b – sl next 2 sts on to cable needle and hold at back, k 3 then p 2 from cable needle; c 6 b – sl next 3 sts on to cable needle and hold at back, k 3 then k 3 from cable needle; c 6 f – sl next 3 sts on to cable needle and hold at front, k 3 then k 3 from cable needle; c 7 dec – sl next 3 sts on to cable needle and hold at front, k 2 tog, k 1, p 1 then k 3 from cable needle; cm – centimetres; cont – continue; dec – decrease; d inc – work k 1 tbl and k 1 into next st, take point of left needle behind work and pick up the strand between the base of the 2

sts just worked and k it tbl; foll – following; in – inches; inc – increase; k – knit; m 1 – make 1 st by picking up strand between sts and k it tbl; p – purl; patt – pattern; psso – pass slipped stitch over; rem – remain(ing); rep – repeat; sl – slip; sl 1 p – slip 1 purl-wise; st(s) – stitch(es); tbl – through back of loop(s); tog – together; wyif – with yarn in front

### NOTE
When working in patt the number of sts varies from row to row where sts are made and lost. When shaping do not include these extra sts in any stitch checks.

### BACK
With 4½ mm needles, cast on 190 sts.
**1st rib row (right side)** K 2, *p 2, k 2; rep from * to end.
**2nd rib row** P 2, *k 2, p 2; rep from * to end.
Rep 1st and 2nd rib rows until back measures 16 cm from cast-on edge, ending with a 1st rib row.
**Dec row** K 4, *k 2 tog, k 10; rep from *

## M·A·R·L·B·O·R·O·U·G·H

14 times, k 2 tog, k 4. 174 sts.
Work foundation rows thus:
**1st row (right side)** P 2, *p 4, k 2, p 4;
rep from * to last 2 sts, p 2.
**2nd row** K 2, *k 4, p 2, k 4; rep from *
to last 2 sts, k 2.
**3rd to 10th rows** Rep 1st and 2nd
rows 4 times.
Cont in patt thus:
**1st row (right side)** P 2, *p 4, k 2, p 5,
d inc, p 2, k 2, p 4; rep from * to last
12 sts, p 4, k 2, p 6.
**2nd row** K 2, *k 4, p 2, k 8, p 2, k 2, p 3,
k 1; rep from * to last 12 sts, k 4, p 2,
k 6.
**3rd row** P 2, *p 4, k 2, p 5, c 4 f, p 1, k 2,
p 2, d inc, p 1; rep from * to last 12 sts,
p 4, k 2, p 6.
**4th row** K 2, *k 4, p 2, k 5, p 3, k 2, p 2,
k 1, p 3, k 2; rep from * to last 12 sts,
k 4, p 2, k 6.
**5th row** P 2, *p 4, k 2, p 6, c 4 f, m 1, k
2, c 5 b, p 1; rep from * to last 12 sts,
p 4, k 2, p 6.
**6th row** K 2, *k 4, p 2, k 7, p 9, k 3; rep
from * to last 12 sts, k 4, p 2, k 6.
**7th row** P 2, *p 4, k 2, p 7, c 6 b, k 3,
p 3; rep from * to last 12 sts, p 4, k 2,
p 6.
**8th row** As 6th.
**9th row** P 2, *p 4, k 2, p 7, k 3, c 6 f, p 3;
rep from * to last 12 sts, p 4, k 2, p 6.
**10th row** As 6th.
**11th row** As 7th.
**12th row** As 6th.
**13th row** P 2, *p 4, k 2, p 5, c 5 b,
c 7 dec, p 2; rep from * to last 12 sts,
p 4, k 2, p 6.
**14th row** K 2, *k 4, p 2, k 6, p 3, k 1, p
2, k 2, wyif sl 1 p, p 2 tog, psso, k 1; rep
from * to last 12 sts, k 4, p 2, k 6.
**15th row** P 2, *p 4, k 2, p 8, k 2, p 1,
k 3, p 2; rep from * to last 12 sts, p 4,
k 2, p 6.
**16th row** K 2, *k 4, p 2, k 6, wyif sl 1 p,
p 2 tog, psso, k 1, p 2, k 4; rep from * to
last 12 sts, k 4, p 2, k 6.
**17th row** P 2, *p 4, k 2, p 4; rep from *
to last 2 sts, p 2.
**18th row** K 2, *k 4, p 2, k 4; rep from *
to last 2 sts, k 2.
**19th row** P 2, *p 1, d inc, p 2,
k 2, p 8, k 2, p 4; rep from * to last 12
sts, p 1,
d inc, p 2, k 2, p 6.
**20th row** K 2, *k 4, p 2, k 2, p 3, k 5,
p 2, k 4; rep from * to last 14 sts, k 4,
p 2, k 2, p 3, k 3.
**21st row** P 2, *p 1, c 4 f, p 1, k 2, p 2, d
inc, p 5, k 2, p 4; rep from * to last 14
sts, p 1, c 4 f, p 1, k 2, p 2, d inc, p 3.

**22nd row** K 2, *k 1, p 3, k 2, p 2, k 1, p
3, k 6, p 2, k 4; rep from * to last 16 sts,
k 1, p 3, k 2, p 2, k 1, p 3, k 4.
**23rd row** P 2, *p 2, c 4 f, m 1, k 2, c 5
b, p 5, k 2, p 4; rep from * to last 16 sts,
p 2, c 4 f, m 1, k 2, c 5 b, p 3.
**24th row** K 2, *k 3, p 9, k 7, p 2, k 4;
rep from * to last 17 sts, k 3, p 9, k 5.
**25th row** P 2, *p 3, c 6 b, k 3, p 7, k 2, p
4; rep from * to last 17 sts, p 3, c 6 b, k
3, p 5.
**26th row** As 24th.
**27th row** P 2, *p 3, k 3, c 6 f, p 7, k 2,
p 4; rep from * to last 17 sts, p 3, k 3,
c 6 f, p 5.
**28th row** As 24th.
**29th row** As 25th.
**30th row** As 24th.

**31st row** P 2, *p 1, c 5 b, c 7 dec, p 6,
k 2, p 4; rep from * to last 17 sts, p 1,
c 5 b, c 7 dec, p 4.
**32nd row** K 2, *k 2, p 3, k 1, p 2, k 2,
wyif sl 1 p, p 2 tog, psso, k 5, p 2, k 4;
rep from * to last 16 sts, k 2, p 3, k 1,
p 2, k 2, wyif sl 1 p, p 2 tog, psso, k 3.
**33rd row** P 2, *p 4, k 2, p 1, k 3, p 6,
k 2, p 4; rep from * to last 14 sts, p 4,
k 2, p 1, k 3, p 4.
**34th row** K 2, *k 2, wyif sl 1 p, p 2 tog,
psso, k 1, p 2, k 8, p 2, k 4; rep from *
to last 14 sts, k 2, wyif sl 1 p, p 2 tog,
psso, k 1, p 2, k 6.
**35th row** As 17th.
**36th row** As 18th.
These 36 rows form patt.
Rep 1st to 36th rows twice, then work

1st to 18th rows again.
Rep 17th and 18th rows.
Cast off loosely in patt.

## POCKET LININGS

**Make 2** With 4½ mm needles, cast on 36 sts.
**1st row** K 1, *p 2, k 2; rep from * to last 3 sts, p 2, k 1.
**2nd row** P 1, *k 2, p 2; rep from * to last 3 sts, k 2, p 1.
Rep 1st and 2nd rows until work measures 15 cm from cast-on edge, ending with a 1st row. Break off yarn and leave sts on a spare needle.

## LEFT FRONT

With 4½ mm needles, cast on 102 sts.
Work 1st and 2nd rib rows of back until rib measures same as back, ending with a 1st rib row.
**Pocket Opening and dec row** *K 6, k 2 tog; rep from * 3 times, k 1, sl next 36 sts on to a stitch holder, k across sts of one pocket lining, k 1, **k 2 tog, k 6; rep from ** 3 times. 94 sts.
Work the 10 foundation rows as back.
Cont in patt thus:
Work 19th to 36th rows, then 1st to 18th rows – thus patt will alternate with back at side seam.

### Front Shaping

Keeping patt correct, beg with 19th row and dec 1 st at end of next row and at same edge on every foll 3rd row until 63 sts rem – note after working 36th row for 4th time, work 35th row again, thus last dec will be on this row. Work 36th row once more. Cast off loosely in patt.

## RIGHT FRONT

Work as left front but work first front dec at beg of row.

## LEFT SLEEVE

With 3¾ mm needles, cast on 50 sts.
Rib 8 cm as at beg of back, ending with a 1st rib row.
**Inc row** K 5, *inc in next st, k 12; rep from * twice, inc in next st, k 5. 54 sts.
Change to 4½ mm needles.
Work 1st and 2nd foundation rows of back 3 times.
Beg with 19th row cont in patt as back, inc 1 st at each end of every wrong-side row until there are 134 sts, taking inc sts into patt.
Patt straight until sleeve measures 44 cm from cast-on edge, ending with a wrong-side row.

### Saddle Shaping

Cast off 55 sts at beg of next 2 rows. 24 sts.
**Inc row** K 3, p 2, *k 2, p twice in next st; rep from * once, k 2, **p twice in next st, k 2; rep from ** once, p 2, k 3. 28 sts.
**Next row** P 3, *k 2, p 2; rep from * to last st, p 1.
**Next row (right side)** K 3, *p 2, k 2; rep from * to last st, k 1.
Rep last 2 rows until saddle extension, when slightly stretched, will fit along front shoulder, ending with a right-side row***.
**Next row** Cast off 1 st, rib 18 including st rem on right needle after casting-off and sl these 18 sts on to a stitch holder, rib to end. Cont in rib on these 9 sts.
Dec 1 st at inner end of the next 7

rows.
Rib rem 2 sts tog and fasten off securely.

## RIGHT SLEEVE

Work as left sleeve to *** but end with a wrong-side row.
Complete to match left sleeve.

## BUTTONHOLE BAND

Leaving centre 44 sts of back free, join saddle extensions to cast-off edges of back and fronts, taking 1 st from each edge of extensions into seam.
With right side facing and using 3¾ mm needles, pick up and k 88 sts evenly up right front edge to beg of front shaping and 76 sts up remainder of front to saddle extension, rib across 18 sts on stitch holder, then pick up and k 27 sts evenly to centre back neck, turn and cast on 1 st. 210 sts.
Beg with 2nd rib row of back, rib 5 rows.
**1st buttonhole row (right side)** Rib 3, cast off next 3 sts, *rib 17 sts including st rem on needle after casting off, cast off next 3 sts; rep from * 3 times, rib to end.
**2nd buttonhole row** Rib to end casting on 3 sts over each cast-off group of 1st row.
Rib 6 rows.
Cast off in rib.

## BUTTON BAND

Work to match buttonhole band, casting on the 1st at beg of pick up row and omitting buttonholes.

## MAKING UP

Join front bands at centre back neck taking 1 st from each edge into seam. With wrong side facing sl 36 sts of pocket on to a 4½ mm needle and cast off knit-wise. Leaving ribbed welts open, join side seams to within 23 cm of cast-off edges of back and fronts. Join sleeve seams, Sew cast-off edges of sleeves into armholes. Sew down pocket linings on wrong side. Sew on buttons.

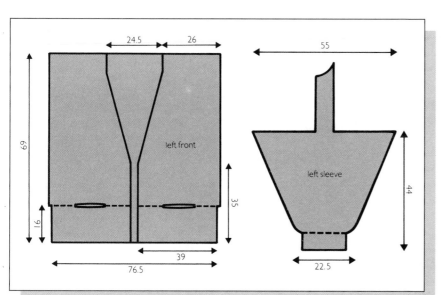

# WINCHESTER

A HUSKY FAIR ISLE IN MUTED NATURAL COLOURS BLENDS PERFECTLY WITH COUNTRY CLOTHES – AND WOULD LOOK JUST AS GOOD ON A MAN. DESIGNED BY TESSA DENNISON

## MATERIALS

Emu Harlech DK Welsh Wool
6 (7) × 50 g balls Bangor (M)
5 (5) × 50 g balls Raglan (A)
5 (6) × 50 g balls Snowdon (B)
2 (2) × 50 g balls Anglesey (C)
Pair each 3¼ mm (No 10) and 4½ mm (No 7) knitting needles

## MEASUREMENTS

To fit bust 86-91 (97-102) cm, 34-36 (38-40) in
Actual measurement – 108 (124) cm, 42½ (49) in
Length – 64 (66) cm
Sleeve length – 44 cm
Figures in brackets are for larger size

## TENSION

24 sts and 24 rows to 10 cm measured over patt on 4½ mm needles

## ABBREVIATIONS

alt – alternate; beg – beginning; cm – centimetres; cont – continue; dec – decreas(e)(ing); foll – following; in – inches; inc – increas(e)(ing); k – knit; m 1 – make 1 st by picking up the strand between sts and k it through the back of the loop; p - purl; patt – pattern; rem – remain(ing); rep – repeat; sl – slip; st(s) – stitch(es); st-st – stocking stitch

## BACK

With 3¼ mm needles and A, cast on 130 (150) sts.
**1st rib row (right side)** K 2, *p 2, k 2; rep from * to end.
Break off A; join M.
**2nd rib row** P 2, *k 2, p 2; rep from * to end.

With M, rep 1st and 2nd rib rows until back measures 8 (10) cm from cast-on edge, ending with a 2nd rib row and inc 1 st at centre of last row. 131 (151) sts. Change to 4½ mm needles.
Cont in st-st from chart, stranding colour not in use loosely across wrong side on two-colour rows thus:
**1st row (right side)** Reading row 1 of chart from right to left, k 20 patt sts 6 (7) times, then k last 11 sts of chart.
**2nd row** Reading row 2 of chart from left to right, p first 11 sts of chart, then p 20 patt sts 6 (7) times.
**3rd to 32nd rows** As 1st and 2nd rows but working rows 3 to 32 of chart. Rep these 32 rows 3 times.

### Neck Shaping

Cont from chart taking care to keep patt correct.
**1st row** Patt 49 (59) sts, turn.
Cont on these sts only for 1st side and leave rem sts on a spare needle.
Cast off 3 sts at beg of next row and on

the foll alt row.
Cont in A. K 1 row. Cast off 3 sts at beg of next row.
Cast off rem 40 (50) sts.
**Next row** With right side facing, sl centre 33 sts on to a stitch holder, rejoin yarn to inner end of rem 49 (59) sts and patt to end.
Patt 1 row.
Cast off 3 sts at beg of next row.
Patt 1 row.
Cont in A.
Cast off 3 sts at beg of next row and on the foll alt row.
Cast off rem 40 (50) sts.

## FRONT

Work as back until the 32 rows of chart have been worked 3 times, then work rows 1 to 16 again.

### Neck Shaping

**1st row** Patt 54 (64) sts, turn.
Cont on these sts only for 1st side and leave rem sts on a spare needle.

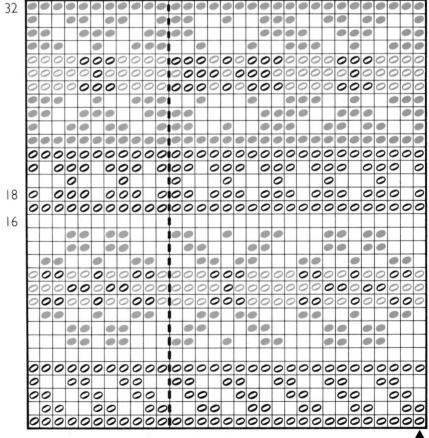

32

18
16

begin here

**KEY**

| B | A | M | C |

pattern

Cast off 3 sts at beg of next row and on the foll 2 alt rows.
Dec 1 st at neck edge on every alt row until 40 (50) sts rem.
Patt straight until front matches back to shoulder.
Cast off.
**Next row:** With right side facing, sl centre 23 sts on to a stitch holder, rejoin yarn to inner end of rem 54 (64) sts and patt to end.
Patt 1 row.
Complete to match 1st side.

### SLEEVES

With 3¼ mm needles and A, cast on 54 (58) sts.

Rib 1 row as back.
Break off A; join M.
Cont in rib until sleeve measures 8 cm from cast-on edge, ending with a 1st rib row.
**Next row** Rib 3 (5), m 1, *rib 3 (4), m 1; rep from * to last 3 (5) sts, rib 3 (5). 71 sts.
Change to 4½ mm needles.
Cont in patt from chart as for back, working the 20 patt sts 3 times and inc 1 st at each end of every 4th row until there are 111 sts, working inc sts into patt. Patt straight until row 21 of chart has been worked for the 3rd time from top of rib. P 1 row with A.
Cast off loosely with A.

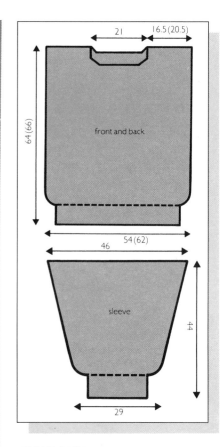

### NECKBAND

Join right shoulder seam.
**1st row** With right side facing, using 3¼ mm needles and A, pick up and k 31 sts evenly down left front neck, k across 23 sts on stitch holder, pick up and k 31 sts up right front neck and 12 sts down right back neck, k across 33 sts on stitch holder then pick up and k 12 sts up left back neck. 142 sts.
**2nd row** P 1 A, reading row 18 of chart from left to right, p 20 patt sts 7 times, p 1 A.
**3rd row** K 1 A, reading row 19 of chart from right to left, k 20 patt sts 7 times, k 1 A.
**4th row** As 2nd row but working row 20 of chart.
**5th row** K with A.
Change to M and p 1 row.
Rib 6 rows as at beg of back.
Change to A and rib 2 rows.
Cast off evenly in rib.

### MAKING UP

Press pieces omitting rib. Join left shoulder and neckband seam. Place markers on side edges of back and front on row 16 of the 3rd rep of chart. With centre of cast-off edge of sleeves to shoulder seams, sew on sleeves between markers. Join side and sleeve seams.

# ETON

THE FISHERMAN'S GUERNSEY GOES SOFT IN CORAL RED COTTON. IT HAS ALL THE EASY FIT OF A SAILING SMOCK. DESIGNED BY SUE TURTON

## MATERIALS
19 × 50 g balls Scheepjeswol Mayflower Helarsgarn
Pair each 3¾ mm (No 9) and 4 mm (No 8) knitting needles
Cable needle

## MEASUREMENTS
One size, to fit up to bust 102 cm, 40 in
Actual measurement – 121 cm, 47½ in
Length – 70 cm
Sleeve length – 42 cm

## TENSION
19 sts and 29 rows to 10 cm over patt of Chart 2 using 4 mm needles

## ABBREVIATIONS
beg – beginning; cm – centimetres; cont – continue; dec – decrease; foll – following; g-st – garter stitch; in – inches; inc – increase; k – knit; m-st – moss stitch; p – purl; patt – pattern; rem – remaining; rep – repeat; sl – slip; st(s) – stitch(es)

## BACK AND FRONT ALIKE
With 3¾ mm needles, cast on 119 sts using thumb method.
Work 6 rows in g-st.
**Inc row** K 6, *inc in next st, k 52; rep from * once, inc in next st, k 6. 122 sts.
Change to 4 mm needles.
Cont in patt thus:
**1st row (right side)** K 3, *reading row 1 of Chart 1 from right to left work 8 sts, reading row 1 of Chart 2 from right to left work 46 sts; rep from * once, reading row 1 of Chart 1 from right to left work 8 sts, k 3.
**2nd row** K 3, *reading row 2 of Chart 1 from left to right work 8 sts, reading row 2 of Chart 2 from left to right work 46 sts; rep from * once, reading

row 2 of Chart 1 from left to right work 8 sts, k 3.
Cont in this way until a total of 190 rows of patt have been worked – note that Chart 1 has 10 rows and Chart 2 has 38 rows; when 10 rows of patt have been worked, cont with row 11 of Chart 2 but beg again at row 1 of Chart 1.

### Neck Shaping
Cont in g-st.
**1st row** K 44 sts, turn.
Cont on these sts only for 1st side.
Dec 1 st at neck edge on the next 4 rows. 40 sts.

K 1 row. Cast off.
**Next row** With right side facing, sl centre 34 sts on to a stitch holder, rejoin yarn to inner end of rem 44 sts and k to end.
Complete to match 1st side.

## SLEEVES
With 3¾ mm needles, cast on 53 sts using thumb method.
Work 6 rows in g-st.
**Inc row** K 26, inc in next st, k 26. 54 sts.
Change to 4 mm needles.
Cont in patt thus:
**1st row (right side)** Reading row 1 of Chart 2 from right to left work sts 1 to

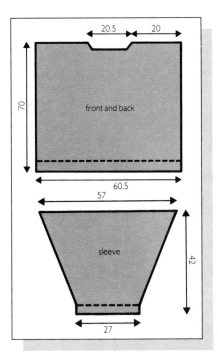

23, reading row I of Chart I from right to left work 8 sts, reading row I of Chart 2 from right to left work sts 24 to 46.

**2nd row** Reading row 2 of Chart 2 from left to right work sts 46 to 24, reading row 2 of Chart I from left to right work 8 sts, reading row 2 of Chart 2 from left to right work sts 23 to I.

Patt 2 rows.

Cont in this way, inc I st at each end of next row and every foll 4th row until there are I I0 sts, working inc sts into moss-st (thus last st of row 6 should be k).

Patt I row, thus a total of I I4 rows of patt have been worked.

P I row.

Cast off loosely knitwise.

## NECKBAND

Join right shoulder seam using a flat seam.

With right side facing and using 3¾ mm needles, pick up and k 9 sts down left front neck, k across 34 sts at centre front, pick up and k 9 sts up right front neck and 9 sts down right back neck, k across 34 sts at centre back then pick up and k 9 sts up left back neck. I04 sts. Work I9 rows in g-st. Cast off loosely.

## MAKING UP

Use flat seams throughout. Join left shoulder and neckband seam. Fold neckband in half on to wrong side and catch stitch loosely in place. With centre of cast-off edge of sleeves to shoulder seams, sew on sleeves. Join side and sleeve seams. Press seams.

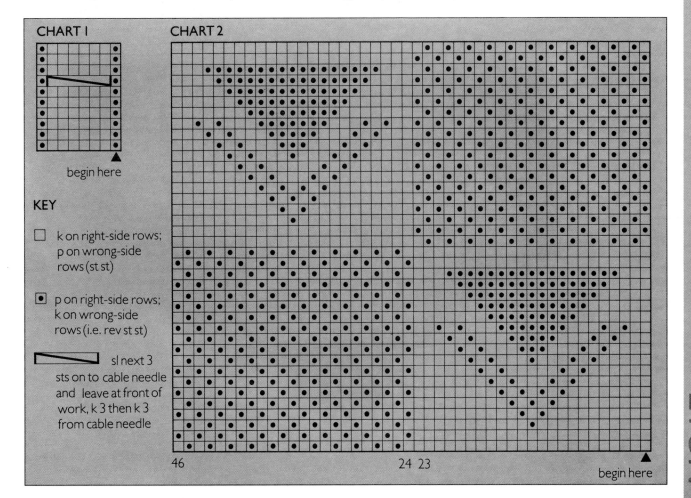

CHART I

begin here

## KEY

☐ k on right-side rows;
p on wrong-side
rows (st st)

◉ p on right-side rows;
k on wrong-side
rows (i.e. rev st st)

▱ sl next 3
sts on to cable needle
and leave at front of
work, k 3 then k 3
from cable needle

CHART 2

46      24 23      begin here

ETON

CLASSIC COLLECTION

# HARROW

A WELL-BRED SWEATER IN A SUBTLY UNTRADITIONAL YARN HAS BEAUTIFUL PROPORTIONS AND LEAFY STITCH DETAIL. DESIGNED BY AILEEN SWAN

## MATERIALS
8 (9, 9) × 50 g balls Schachenmayr Stella
Pair each 2¾ mm (No 12) and 3¼ mm (No 10) knitting needles
Cable needle
Shoulder pads

## MEASUREMENTS
To fit bust 81 (86, 91) cm, 32 (34, 36) in
Actual measurement – 85 (91, 97) cm, 33½ (36, 38) in
Length – 54 cm
Sleeve length – 45 cm
Figures in round brackets are for larger sizes

## TENSION
Based on a st-st tension of 24 sts and 32 rows to 10 cm on 3¼ mm needles.
30 sts of chart measure 10.5 cm

## ABBREVIATIONS
alt – alternate; beg – beginning; cm – centimetres; cont – continue; dec – decrease; foll – following; in – inches; inc – increase; k – knit; p – purl; patt – pattern; rem – remain(ing); rep – repeat; sl – slip; st(s) – stitch(es); st-st – stocking stitch; tbl – through back of loop; tog – together
Work instructions in square brackets the number of times given

## BACK
With 2¾ mm needles, cast on 105 (113, 121) sts.
**1st rib row (right side)** K 1 tbl, *p 1, k 1 tbl; rep from * to end.
**2nd rib row** P 1 tbl, *k 1, p 1 tbl; rep from * to end.
Rep 1st and 2nd rib rows 9 times, then work 1st rib row again.

**Inc row** K 1, inc in next st, *p 1 tbl, [inc in next st, p 1 tbl] 2 (3, 4) times, rib 6, inc in next st, [rib 3, inc in next st] twice, rib 12; rep from * twice, p 1 tbl, [inc in next st, p 1 tbl] 2 (3, 4) times, inc in next st, k 1. 124 (136, 148) sts.
Change to 3¼ mm needles.
Cont in patt thus:
**1st row (right side)** P 3, *k 1 tbl, [p 2, k 1 tbl] 2 (3, 4) times, reading row 1 of chart from right to left work 30 sts; rep from * twice, k 1 tbl, [p 2, k 1 tbl] 2 (3, 4) times, p 3.
**2nd row** K 3, *p 1 tbl, [k 2, p 1 tbl] 2 (3, 4) times, reading row 2 of chart from left to right work 30 sts; rep from * twice, p 1 tbl, [k 2, p 1 tbl] 2 (3, 4) times, k 3.
These 2 rows establish rib patt between and at each side of chart panels.
Cont in this way until each chart row has been worked.
These 36 rows form patt.
Cont in patt until row 20 (18, 16) of the 3rd patt from beg has been worked.

### Armhole Shaping
Keeping patt correct, cast off 7 (9, 11) sts at beg of next 2 rows.
Dec 1 st at each end of next row and on the foll 4 (5, 6) alt rows. 100 (106, 112) sts**.
Patt straight until row 8 of the 5th patt from beg has been worked.

### Shoulder and Neck Shaping
**1st row** Cast off 8 (9, 10) sts, patt until there are 28 (29, 30) sts on right needle, turn. Cont on these sts only leaving rem sts on a spare needle.
**2nd row** Cast off 5 sts, patt to end.
**3rd row** Cast off 8 (9, 10) sts, patt to end.
**4th row** As 2nd.
Cast off rem 10 sts.
**Next row** With right side facing, sl centre 28 (30, 32) sts on to a stitch holder, rejoin yarn to inner end of rem 36 (38, 40) sts and patt to end.
Cast off 8 (9, 10) sts at beg of next row.
Beg with 2nd row, complete to match 1st side.

## FRONT
Work as back to **.
Patt straight until row 18 of the 4th patt from beg has been worked.

### Neck Shaping
**1st row** Patt 39 (41, 43) sts, turn.
Cont on these sts only leaving rem sts on a spare needle.
***Cast off 2 sts at beg of next row and on the foll 3 alt rows. Dec 1 st at beg of next 5 alt rows. 26 (28, 30) sts.
Patt 8 rows straight.

### Shoulder Shaping
Cast off 8 (9, 10) sts at beg of next row and on the foll alt row.
Patt 1 row. Cast off rem 10 sts.
**Next row** With right side facing, sl centre 22 (24, 26) sts on to a stitch holder, rejoin yarn to inner end of rem 39 (41, 43) sts and patt to end.
Patt 1 row.
Complete to match 1st side from ***

## SLEEVES
With 2¾ mm needles, cast on 49 (53, 57) sts.
Rib 19 (21, 23) rows as at beg of back.
**Inc row** K 1, [inc in next st, p 1 tbl] 5 (6, 7) times, rib 6, inc in next st, [rib 3, inc in next st] twice, rib 12, [p 1 tbl, inc in next st] 5 (6, 7) times, k 1. 62 (68, 74) sts.
Change to 3¼ mm needles.
Cont in patt thus:
**1st row (right side)** P 3, k 1 tbl, [p 2, k 1 tbl] 4 (5, 6) times, reading from right to left work 30 sts of row 1 of chart, [k 1 tbl, p 2] 4 (5, 6) times, k 1 tbl, p 3.
**2nd row** K 3, p 1 tbl, [k 2, p 1 tbl] 4 (5, 6) times, reading from left to right work 30 sts of row 2 of chart, [p 1 tbl, k 2] 4 (5, 6) times, p 1 tbl, k 3.
Cont in patt in this way, inc 1 st at each end of 5th row and every foll 8th row until there are 86 (92, 98) sts, taking inc sts into rib at each side.
Patt straight until row 20 (18, 16) of the 4th patt from beg has been worked.

### Top Shaping
Cast off 7 (9, 11) sts at beg of next 2 rows. Dec 1 st at each end of next row and every foll alt row until 56 sts rem.
Dec 1 st at each end of every 4th row until 44 sts rem. Dec 1 st at each end of every row until 30 sts rem.
**Next row** P 2 tog to end.
**Next row** *K 1, k 2 tog; rep from * to end.
Cast off rem 10 sts.

## NECKBAND
Join right shoulder seam.
With right side facing and using 2¾ mm needles, pick up and k 31 (32, 31) sts evenly down left front neck, across

CLASSIC COLLECTION

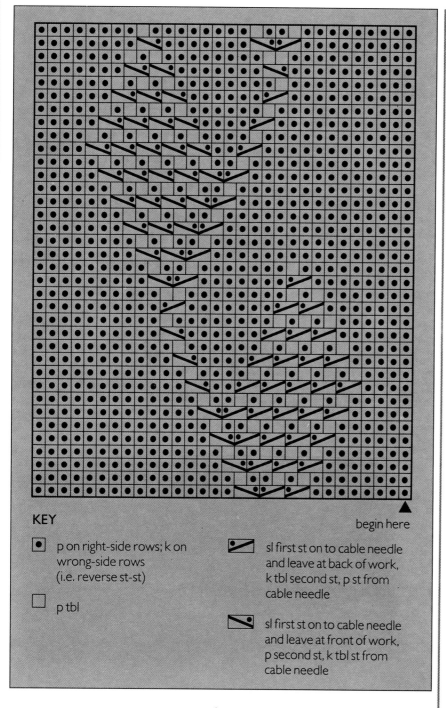

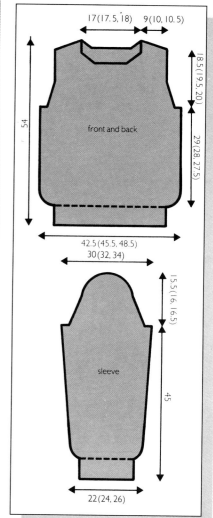

### KEY

⊡ p on right-side rows; k on wrong-side rows (i.e. reverse st-st)

☐ p tbl

begin here

⬛╱ sl first st on to cable needle and leave at back of work, k tbl second st, p st from cable needle

⬛╲ sl first st on to cable needle and leave at front of work, p second st, k tbl st from cable needle

centre sts work, p 13 (14, 15), k 1 tbl, p 2 tog, k 1 tbl, p 5 (6, 7); pick up and k 31 (32, 31) sts up right front neck and 15 (14, 15) sts down right back neck; across centre sts work, p 4 (5, 6), [k 1 tbl, p 1] 4 times, k 1 tbl, p 2 tog, k 1 tbl, p 12 (13, 14); pick up and k 15 (14, 15) sts up left back neck then cast on 1 st for seam. 141 (145, 149) sts.
Beg with 2nd rib row, rib 6 cm as at beg of back.
Cast off very loosely in rib.

### MAKING UP
Join left shoulder and neckband seam.

Fold neckband in half on to wrong side and catch stitch loosely in place. Set in sleeves. Taking 1½ sts from each edge into seams, join side and sleeve seams. Sew in shoulder pads.

# BLUE JEAN BABY

# DENIM DAYS

STORMY SKY COLOURS AND DENSE ARAN STITCHES COMBINE TO PRODUCE A RUGGED OUTDOOR SWEATER, DESTINED TO BECOME A FUTURE CLASSIC. DESIGNED BY CAROLINE INGRAM

## MATERIALS
Robin Pure New Wool Aran:
17 × 50 g balls shade Danube (M)
3 × 50 g balls shade Marine (A)
2 × 50 g balls shade Como (B)
Pair each 3¾ mm (No 9) and 4½ mm
(No 7) knitting needles
Cable needle

## MEASUREMENTS
One size, to fit up to bust 97 cm, 38 in
Actual measurement – 106 cm, 42 in
approx
Length – 61 cm approx
Sleeve length – 43 cm approx

## TENSION
20 sts and 30 rows to 10 cm measured
over m-st on 4½ mm needles

## ABBREVIATIONS
alt – alternate; beg – beginning; c 4 b –
slip next 2 sts on to cable needle and
hold at back, k 2 then k 2 from cable
needle; c 4 f – slip next 2 sts on to cable
needle and hold at front, k 2 then k 2
from cable needle; c 3 b – slip next st
on to cable needle and hold at back, k 2
then p st from cable needle; c 3 f – slip
next 2 sts on to cable needle and hold
at front of work, p 1 then k 2 from
cable needle; c 5 b – slip next 3 sts on
to cable needle and hold at back, k 2,
slip last st from cable needle to left
hand needle and p this st, then k 2 from
cable needle; cm – centimetres; cont –
continue; dec – decrease; foll –
following; in – inches; inc – increase; k –
knit; m 1 – make 1 st by picking up the
strand between sts and k it through the
back of the loop; m b – make bobble
by working [k 1, p 1] 3 times, k 1 into
next st (7 sts), then pass 2nd, 3rd, 4th,
5th, 6th, 7th sts over 1st st; m-st – moss
stitch; patt – pattern; p – purl; rem –
remaining; rep – repeat; sl – slip; st(s) –
stitch(es); tog – together

## BACK
With 3¾ mm needles and M, cast on
113 sts.
**1st row (right side)** P 1, *k 1, p 1; rep
from * to end.
**2nd row** K 1, *p 1, k 1; rep from * to
end.
Rep these 2 rows 7 times, then work
1st row again.
**Inc row** Rib 2, m 1, rib 4, m 1, rib 6, m
1, rib 13, m 1, rib 4, m 1, rib 7, m 1, rib
7, m 1, rib 6, m 1, rib 15, m 1, rib 6, m 1,
rib 7, m 1, rib 7, m 1, rib 4, m 1, rib 13,
m 1, rib 6, m 1, rib 4, m 1, rib 2. 129 sts.
Change to 4½ mm needles.
Cont in patt thus, using M except
where indicated otherwise and
twisting yarns at colour changes:
**1st row (right side)** [K 1, p 1] 5 times,
work 1st row of panel 1, work 1st row
of panel 2, work 1st row of panel 3, [p
1, k 1] twice, **work 1st row of panel
4, [k 1, p 1] twice, work 1st row of

panel 1, work 1st row of panel 5, work
1st row of panel 3, [p 1, k 1] twice,
work 1st row of panel 4, **[k 1, p 1]
twice, work 1st row of panel 1, work
1st row of panel 2, work 1st row of
panel 3, [p 1, k 1] 5 times.
**2nd row** [K 1, p 1] 4 times, k 2, work
2nd row of panel 3, work 2nd row of
panel 2, work 2nd row of panel 1, k 2,
p 1, k 1, **work 2nd row of panel 4,
k 1, p 1, k 2, work 2nd row of panel 3,
work 2nd row of panel 5, work 2nd
row of panel 1, k 2, p 1, k 1, work 2nd
row of panel 4, **k 1, p 1, k 2, work
2nd row of panel 3, work 2nd row of
panel 2, work 2nd row of panel 1, k 2,
[p 1, k 1] 4 times.
These 2 rows set position of panels
and m-st.
Cont to patt as set from 3rd row of
panels. Rep each panel as it is
completed.
Patt straight until work measures 38
cm approx, ending with 14th row of
4th rep of panel 5.

### Armhole Shaping
Cast off 8 sts at beg of next 2 rows.

113 sts.***
Keeping patt correct, cont straight until back measures 61 cm approx, ending with last row of 6th rep of panel 5.
**Next row** Cast off 29 sts, sl next 55 sts on to a stitch holder, rejoin yarn to inner end of rem 29 sts.
Cast off.

## FRONT

Work as back to ***.
Keeping patt correct, cont straight until front measures 51 cm approx, ending with 24th row of 5th rep of panel 5.

### Neck Shaping

**1st row** Patt 46, turn.
Cont on these sts only for 1st side and leave rem sts on a spare needle.
Dec 1 st at neck edge on next 17 rows. 29 sts.
Patt 14 rows straight.
Cast off.
**Next row** With right side facing, sl centre 21 sts on to a stitch holder, rejoin yarn to inner end of rem 46 sts and patt to end.
Complete to match 1st side.

## SLEEVES

Using 3¾ mm needles and M, cast on 45 sts.
Work 17 rows rib as for back.
**Inc row (wrong side)** Rib 3, *m 1, rib 3; rep from * to end. 59 sts.
Change to 4½ mm needles.
Cont in patt thus, using M except where indicated otherwise:
**1st row** P 1, k 1, work from ** to ** of 1st row of back, k 1, p 1.
**2nd row** P 1, k 1, work from ** to ** of 2nd row of back, k 1, p 1.
These 2 rows set position of panels and m-st.
Cont to patt as set, AT THE SAME TIME inc 1 st at each end of next and foll 4th rows, working extra sts in m-st, until there are 105 sts.
Patt straight until sleeve measures 47 cm approx, ending with 14th row of 5th rep of panel 5.
Cast off.

## NECKBAND

Join right shoulder seam.
With 3¾ mm needles and M, pick up and k 27 sts evenly down left front neck, k 10, k 2 tog, k 9 across 21 sts at centre front, pick up and k 27 sts up right front neck then k 13, *k 2 tog, k 12; rep from * to end across 55 sts

of back neck. 126 sts.
Work 9 rows k 1, p 1 rib. Cast off in rib.

## MAKING UP

Join left shoulder and neckband seam.
With centre of cast-off edge of sleeves to shoulder seams and straight edges of sleeves to cast-off sts of armholes, set in sleeves. Join side and sleeve seams. Press seams.

### PANEL 1 (4 sts)
**1st row** K 2, k 2 A.
**2nd row** P 2 A, p 2.
**3rd row** C 4 b, working colours as set.
**4th row** P 2, p 2 A.
**5th row** K 2 A, k 2.
**6th row** As 4th.
**7th row** C 4 b, working colours as set.
**8th row** As 2nd.

### PANEL 2 (15 sts)
**1st row** P 5, k 2, m b A, k 2, p 5.
**2nd row** K 5, p 5, k 5.
**3rd row** P 5, [k 1, m b A] twice, k 1, p 5.
**4th row** As 2nd.
**5th row** As 1st.
**6th row** As 2nd.
**7th row** P 4, c 3 b, p 1, c 3 f, p 4.
**8th row** K 4, p 2, k 1, p 1, k 1, p 2, k 4.
**9th row** P 3, c 3 b, k 1, p 1, k 1, c 3 f, p 3.
**10th row** K 3, p 3, k 1, p 1, k 1, p 3, k 3.
**11th row** P 2, c 3 b, [p 1, k 1] twice, p 1, c 3 f, p 2.
**12th row** K 2, p 2, [k 1, p 1] 3 times, k 1, p 2, k 2.
**13th row** P 2, k 3, [p 1, k 1] twice, p 1, k 3, p 2.
**14th row** K 2, p 2, [k 1, p 1] 3 times, k 1, p 2, k 2.
**15th row** P 2, c 3 f, [p 1, k 1] twice, p 1, c 3 b, p 2.
**16th row** K 3, p 3, k 1, p 1, k 1, p 3, k 3.
**17th row** P 3, c 3 f, k 1, p 1, k 1, c 3 b, p 3.
**18th row** K 4, p 2, k 1, p 1, k 1, p 2, k 4.
**19th row** P 4, c 3 f, p 1, c 3 b, p 4.
**20th row** K 5, p 5, k 5.
**21st to 40th rows** Rep 1st to 20th rows but work bobbles with B.

### PANEL 3 (4 sts)
**1st row** K 2, k 2 A.
**2nd row** P 2 A, p 2.
**3rd row** C 4 f, working colours as set.
**4th row** P 2, p 2 A.
**5th row** K 2 A, k 2.
**6th row** As 4th.
**7th row** C 4 f, working colours as set.
**8th row** As 2nd.

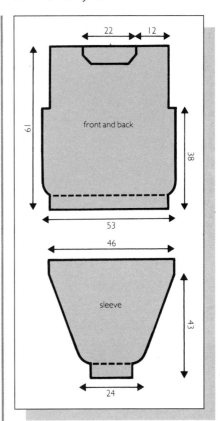

### PANEL 4 (9 sts)
**1st row** K 9.
**2nd row** P 9.
**3rd row** C 4 b, k 1, c 4 f.
**4th row** P 9.
**5th row** K 4, m b B, k 4.
**6th row** P 9.
**7th and 8th rows** As 1st and 2nd rows.

### PANEL 5 (21 sts)
**1st row** P 8, c 5 b, p 8.
**2nd row** K 8, p 2, k 1, p 2, k 8.
**3rd row** P 7, c 3 b, p 1, c 3 f, p 7.
**4th row** K 7, p 2, k 3, p 2, k 7.
**5th row** P 6, c 3 b, p 1, m b B, p 1, c 3 f, p 6.
**6th row** K 6, p 2, k 5, p 2, k 6.
**7th row** P 5, c 3 b, [p 1, m b B] twice, p 1, c 3 f, p 5.
**8th row** K 5, p 2, k 7, p 2, k 5.
**9th row** P 4, c 3 b, [p 1, m b B] 3 times, p 1, c 3 f, p 4.
**10th row** K 4, p 2, k 9, p 2, k 4.
**11th row** P 3, c 3 b, p 2, k 2, p 1, k 2, p 2, c 3 f, p 3.
**12th row** [K 3, p 2] twice, k 1, [p 2, k 3] twice.
**13th row** P 2, c 3 b, p 3, k 2, p 1, k 2, p 3, c 3 f, p 2.
**14th row** K 2, p 2, k 4, p 2, k 1, p 2, k 4, p 2, k 2.
**15th to 28th rows** Rep 1st to 14th rows but work bobbles with A.

B·O·K·H·A·R·A

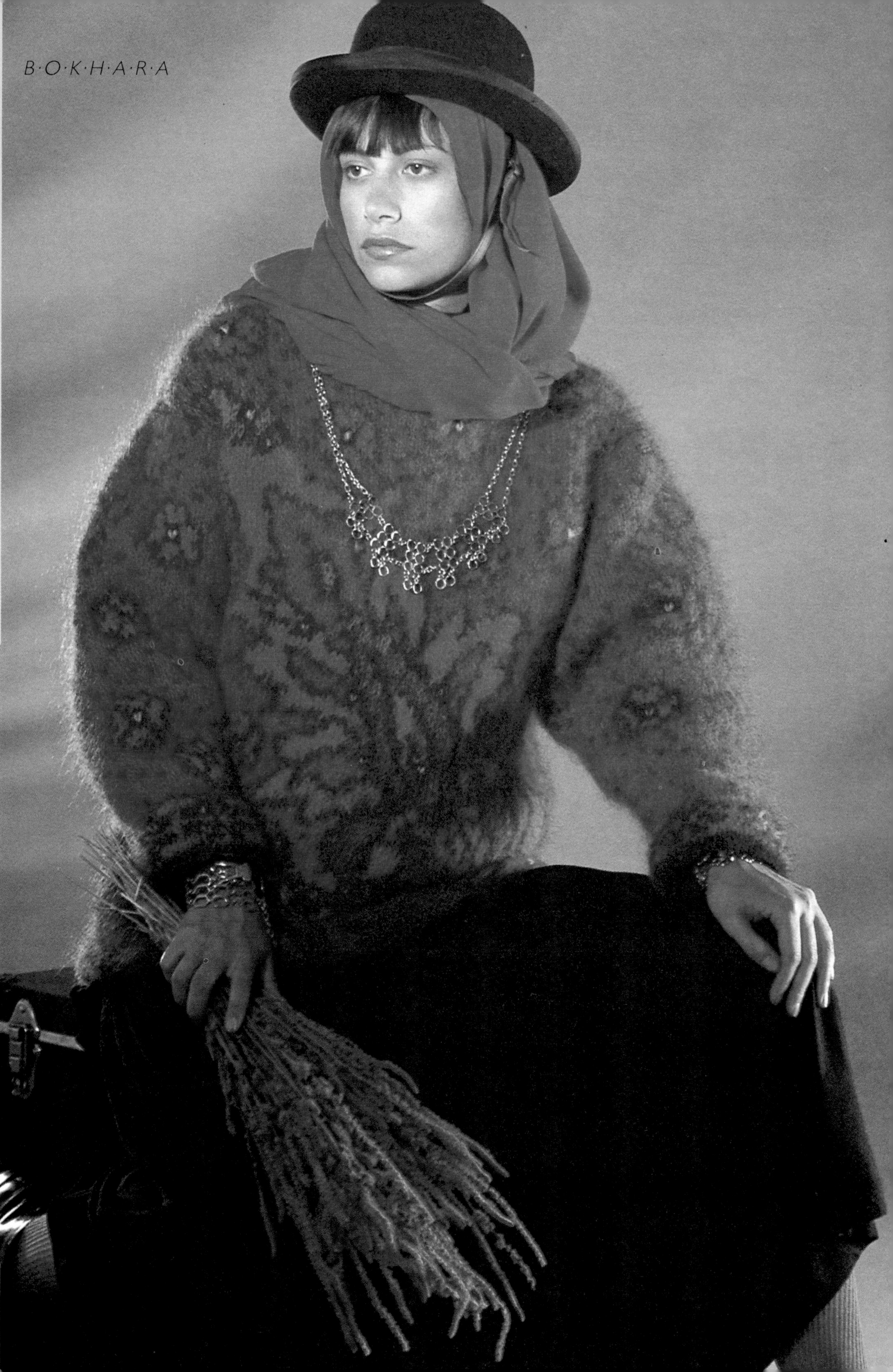

# TURKESTAN

## BOKHARA

AN EXOTIC COMBINATION OF RICH COLOUR AND FOLK-INSPIRED PATTERNS, THIS HUGE MOHAIR SWEATER IS ALMOST A TUNIC, TAPERING TO A BROAD BAND AT THE HIP. DESIGNED BY MELODY GRIFFITHS

### MATERIALS
Sunbeam Paris Mohair
11 × 25 g balls shade Electric (M)
11 × 25 g balls shade Storm (A)
5 × 25 g balls shade Sunshade (B)
2 × 25 g balls shade Neptune (C)
1 × 25 g ball  shade Gold Dust (D)
Pair each 5 mm (No 6) and 5½ mm (No 5) knitting needles

### MEASUREMENTS
One size, to fit up to bust 97 cm, 38 in
Actual measurement – 121 cm, 47½ in
Length – 74 cm, 29 in
Sleeve length – 47 cm, 18½ in

### TENSION
17 sts and 17 rows to 10 cm measured over patt on 5½ mm needles

### ABBREVIATIONS
beg – beginning; cm – centimetres; cont – continue; dec – decrease; foll – following; in – inches; inc – increase; k – knit; p – purl; patt – pattern; rem – remaining; sl – slip; st(s) – stitch(es); st-st – stocking stitch; tog – together

### NOTE
This garment uses three methods of working with colour.
Charts 1 and 3 are worked in traditional Fair Isle technique. Charts 2 and 4 are worked in a combination of Fair Isle for shades Electric and Storm with motif knitting for Sunshade and Neptune. Do not strand Sunshade and Neptune all the way across back of work. The single Gold Dust sts are Swiss Darned after pieces are completed – they should be knitted in Storm
Charts 2 and 4 are in two halves; in each case the two halves should be read as one.

### BACK
With 5½ mm needles and A, cast on

27 sts for hip band.
Work in st–st from Chart 1 thus:
1st row is a k row, read chart from right to left.
2nd row is a p row, read chart from left to right.
Cont from chart in this way until all 81 rows have been worked.
Cast off purl-wise with A.
With right side facing, join A to 1st st of 1st row then pick up and k 83 sts evenly along row-ends of hip band to cast-on edge.
Work in st-st from Chart 2 thus:
1st row is a p row, read chart from left to right.
2nd row is a k row, read chart from right to left.

*B·O·K·H·A·R·A*

**CHART 1**

**CHART 2**

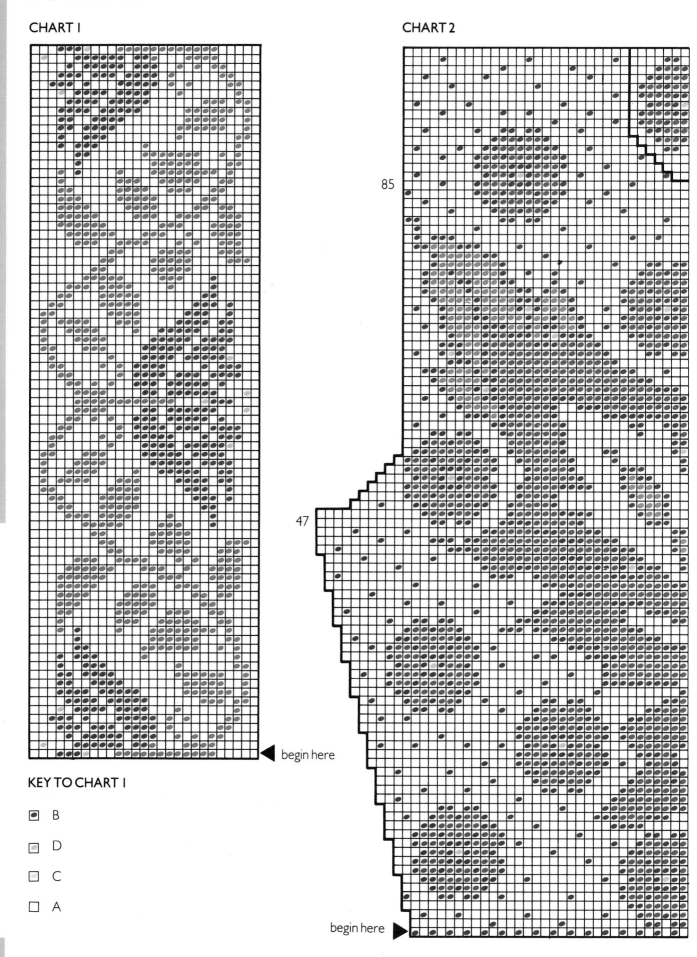

85

47

begin here ◀

begin here ▶

**KEY TO CHART 1**

- ⊡ B
- ⊡ D
- ☐ C
- ☐ A

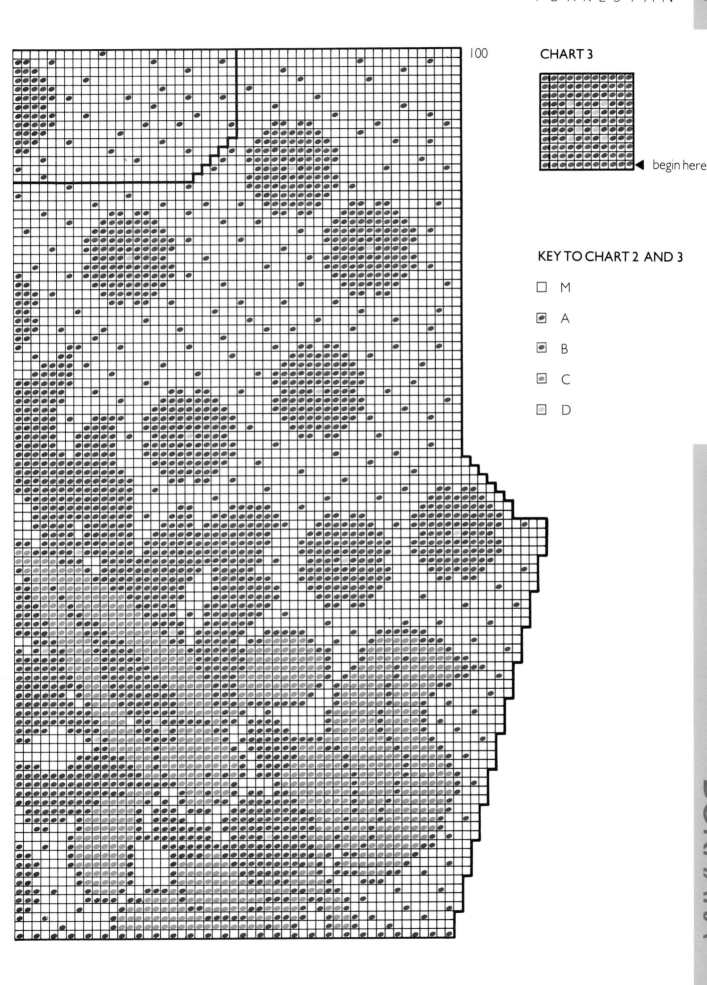

CHART 3

◄ begin here

KEY TO CHART 2 AND 3

☐ M

☒ A

☒ B

☒ C

☒ D

100

*B·O·K·H·A·R·A*

## CHART 4

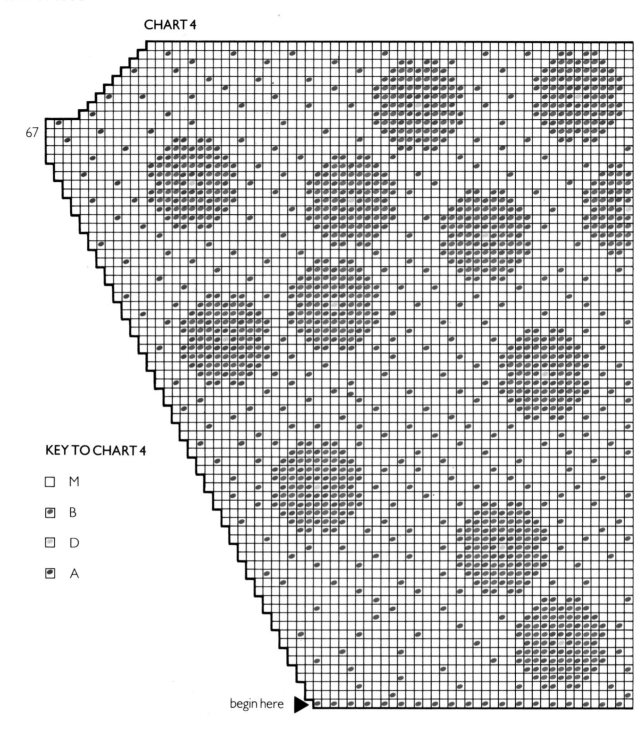

67

### KEY TO CHART 4

☐  M

▨  B

▨  D

▨  A

begin here ▶

---

Cont from chart in this way, inc 1 st at each end of 4th row of chart and every foll 4th row as shown, until there are 105 sts.
Patt 3 rows straight, thus completing 47 rows of chart.

### Armhole Shaping
Cont from chart, casting off 4 sts at beg of next 2 rows.
Dec 1 st at each end of next 6 rows.

85 sts.
Cont straight from chart until all 100 rows have been completed. Cast off with M.

### FRONT
Work as back until 85 rows of chart have been completed.

### Neck Shaping
Cont from chart thus:

**Next row (right side)** Patt 31 sts, turn.
Cont on these sts only for 1st side and leave rem sts on a spare needle.
Dec 1 st at neck edge on the next 5 rows. 26 sts.
Cont straight from chart until all 100 rows have been completed. Cast off with M.
**Next row** With right side facing, sl centre 23 sts on to a stitch holder, rejoin yarn to inner end of rem 31 sts

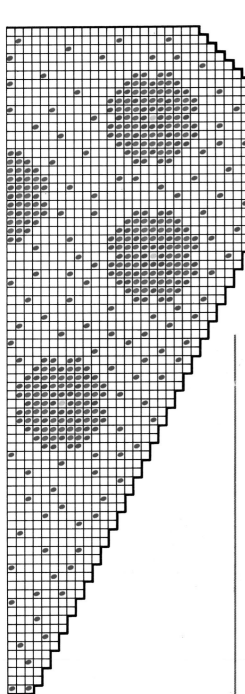

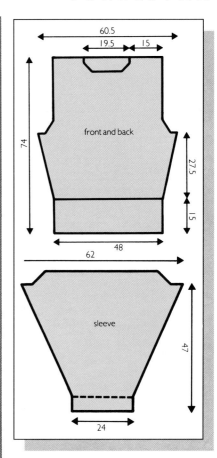

before dotted line 4 times, then k st after dotted line.

**2nd row** Reading 2nd row of chart from left to right, p st before dotted line then p the 10 sts after dotted line 4 times.

Cont from chart in this way until all 11 rows have been worked. P 1 row with A.

Fold work in half with cast-on edge behind sts on needle.

**Next row (close hem)** With A, *k next st from needle tog with corresponding st from cast-on edge; rep from * to end.

Work in st-st from Chart 4 thus:
1st row is a p row, read chart from left to right.
2nd row is a k row, read chart from right to left, inc at each end of row as shown.

Cont from chart in this way, inc 1 st at each end of every k row until there are 105 sts. Patt 3 rows straight, thus completing 67 rows of chart.

## Top Shaping
Cast off 4 sts at beg of next 2 rows.
Dec 1 st at each end of next 8 rows.
81 sts.
Cast off loosely with M.

## NECKBAND
Mark centre 33 sts on cast-off edge of back for neck.
Join right shoulder seam.
With 5½ mm needles and A, pick up and k 18 sts evenly down left front neck, k across 23 sts at centre front,

pick up and k 18 sts up right front neck and 32 sts across back neck. 91 sts.
P 1 row.

Cont in st-st from Chart 3 thus:
**1st row (right side)** Reading 1st row of chart from right to left, k the 10 sts before dotted line 9 times, then k st after dotted line.

**2nd row** Reading 2nd row of chart from left to right, p st before dotted line then p the 10 sts after dotted line 9 times.

Cont from chart in this way until all 11 rows have been worked.
P 2 rows with A.
Change to 5 mm needles.
Beg with a p row, st-st 10 rows with A.
Fold neckband in half on to wrong side and * loosely sew 1 st from needle to corresponding st of pick up row; rep from * to end.

## MAKING UP
Press lightly. Join left shoulder and neckband seam – join outer and inner edges of neckband separately. With centre of cast-off edge of sleeves to shoulder seams, set in sleeves. Join side seams carefully matching patt on hip bands. Join sleeve seams joining outer and inner edges of cuffs separately.

and patt to end.
Complete to match 1st side.

## SLEEVES
With 5 mm needles and A, cast on 41 sts for cuff.
St-st 12 rows.
Change to 5½ mm needles. P 2 rows.
Cont in st-st from Chart 3 thus:
**1st row (right side)** Reading 1st row of chart from right to left, k the 10 sts

# TASHKENT

**S**TYLISED EASTERN FLOWERS SPREAD OVER A BIG MOHAIR JACKET AND DRAW ATTENTION TO SHOULDERS. DESIGNED BY LESLEY STANFIELD

## MATERIALS

Argyll Finesse Mohair
18 × 25 g balls Mandrake (M)
3 × 25 g balls Sirocco (A)
3 × 25 g balls Raspberry (B)
3 × 25 g balls Aubretia (C)
1 × 25 g ball Antique Gold (D)
Pair each 5½ mm (No 5) and 6½ mm (No 3) knitting needles
Pair large detachable shoulder pads

## MEASUREMENTS

One size, to fit up to bust 107 cm, 42 in
Actual measurement – 134 cm, 52½ in approx
Length – 77 cm approx
Sleeve length – 32 cm approx

## TENSION

13 sts and 17 rows to 10 cm over st-st on 6½ mm needles

## ABBREVIATIONS

alt – alternate; beg – beginning; cm – centimetres; cont– continue; dec –decrease; foll – following; in – inches; inc – increase; k – knit; p – purl; patt – pattern; psso – pass slipped stitch over; rem – remain(ing); rep – repeat; sl – slip; st(s) – stitch(es); st-st – stocking stitch; tbl – through back of loops

## BACK

With 5½ mm needles and M, cast on 89 sts.
Beg k, work 7 rows in st-st.
K 1 row to mark hemline.
Change to 6½ mm needles.
Cont in st-st from Chart 1, stranding colour(s) not in use loosely across wrong side on multi-colour rows, thus:
**1st row (right side)** Reading row 1 of chart from right to left, k 8 patt sts 11 times, then k last st.

**2nd row** Reading row 2 of chart from left to right, p first st, then p 8 patt sts 11 times.
**3rd to 8th rows** As 1st and 2nd rows but working rows 3 to 8 of chart *.
Cont in st-st from Chart 2, reading rows alternately from right to left, then left to right. Only strand colour not in use across small areas (eg some stems). Otherwise, work with separate lengths of yarns, twisting them at each colour change (see colour knitting notes on page . Small areas of colour may be Swiss darned afterwards, if preferred.
Cont until row 56 has been completed.

### Raglan Shaping

Cont from chart, dec 1 st at each end of row 57 and every foll alt row until row 98 has been completed (work k 2 tog at beg and k 2 tog tbl at end for each dec). 47 sts.
Cont from chart, dec 1 st at each end of every row until row 110 has been completed. Leave rem 23 sts on a stitch holder.

### LEFT FRONT

With 5½ mm needles and M, cast on 41 sts.
Work as back to * but work the patt sts 5 times **.
Work rows 1 to 56 of Chart 3.

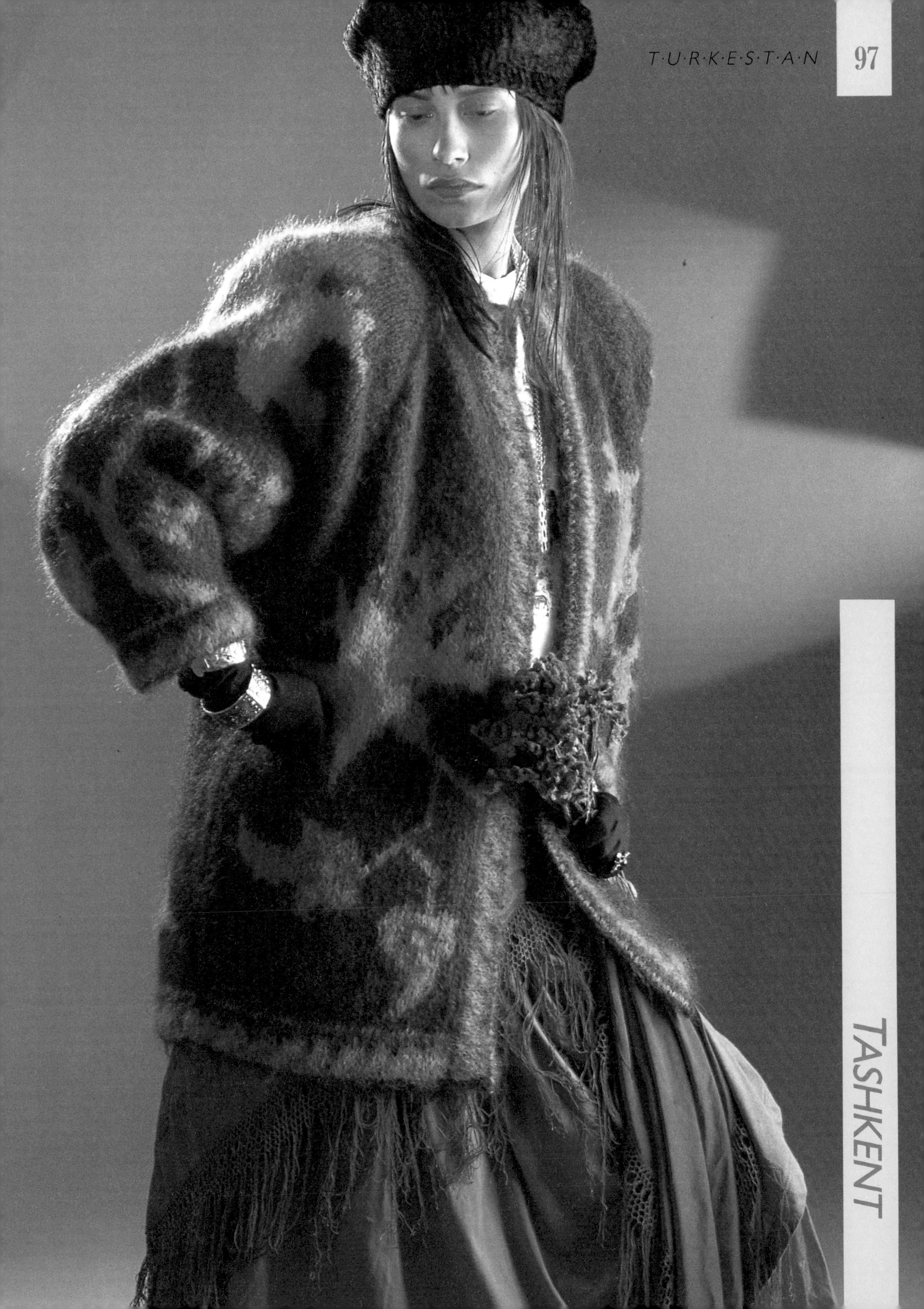

TASHKENT

T·A·S·H·K·E·N·T

**CHART I**

**CHART 2**

**KEY TO ALL CHARTS**

110

56

begin here

□ M

▨ A

▨ B

▨ C

▨ D

begin here

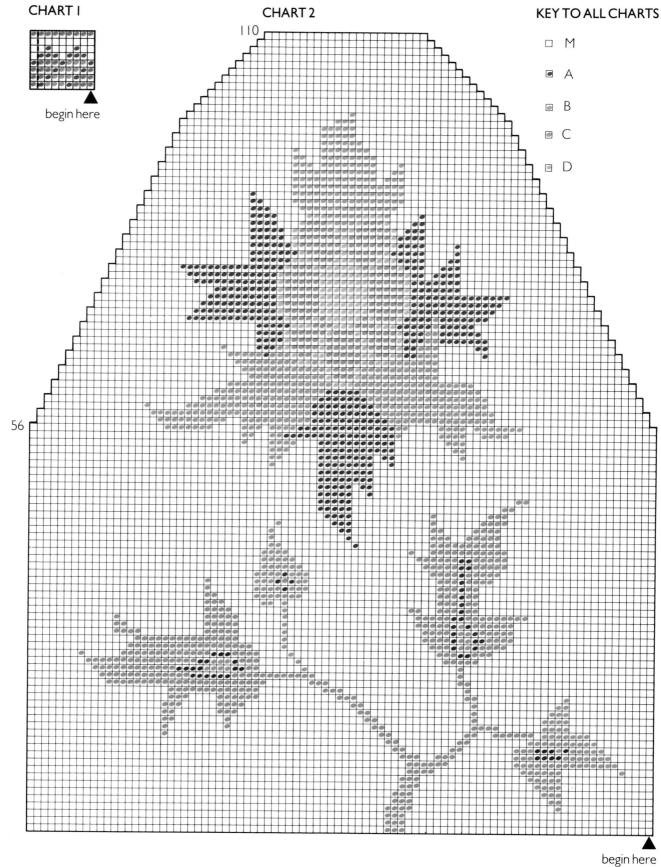

CHART 4  CHART 3

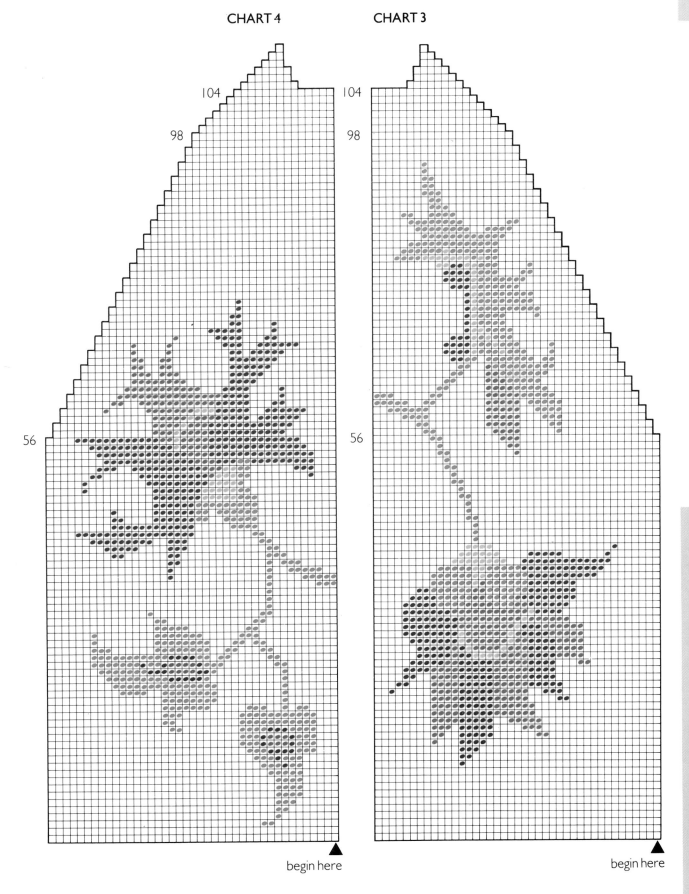

104  104
98  98
56  56

begin here  begin here

*T·A·S·H·K·E·N·T*

**Raglan Shaping**

Cont from chart, dec 1 st at beg of row 57 and every foll alt row until row 98 has been completed. 20 sts.
Dec 1 st at raglan edge on every row until row 104 has been completed. 14 sts.
**105th row** K 2 tog, k 7, sl rem 5 sts on to a safety pin.
***Dec 1 st at neck edge on next row and on the foll alt row, AND AT THE

SAME TIME, dec 1 st at raglan edge on every row until 2 sts rem.
P 2 tog and fasten off.

**RIGHT FRONT**
Work as left front to **.
Work rows 1 to 56 of Chart 4.

**Raglan Shaping**
Cont from chart, dec 1 st at end of row

57 and every foll alt row until row 98 has been completed. 20 sts.
Dec 1 st at raglan edge on every row until row 104 has been completed. 14 sts.
**105th row** Break yarn, sl 5 sts on to a safety pin, rejoin yarn and k 7, k 2 tog tbl.
Complete to match left front from ***.

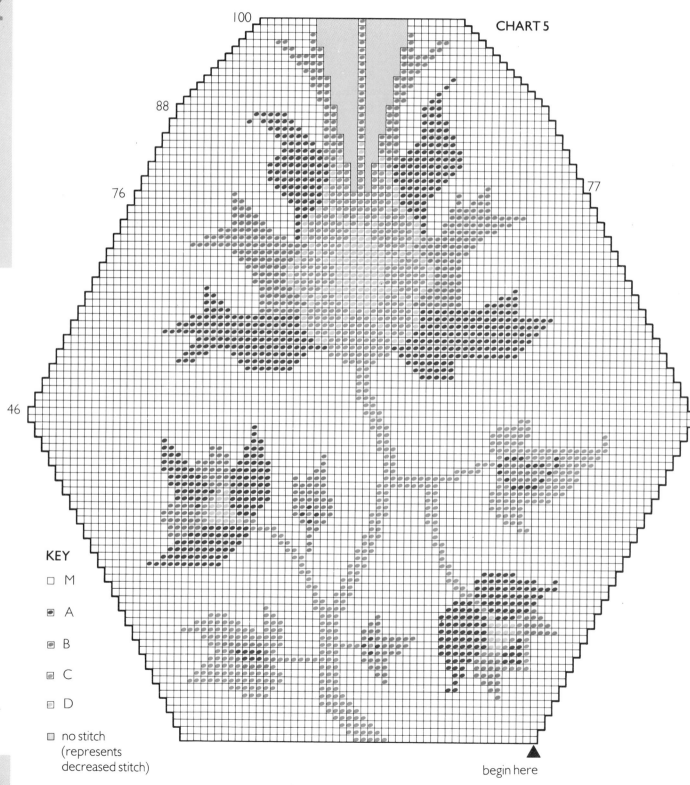

CHART 5

KEY

☐ M

▨ A

▨ B

▨ C

▨ D

☐ no stitch (represents decreased stitch)

begin here

## SLEEVES

With 5½ mm needles and M, cast on 49 sts. Work as back to * but work the 8 patt sts 6 times.

Cont in st-st from Chart 5, inc 1 st at each end of row 1 and every foll alt row (row 1 of 51 sts includes increases). Cont from chart until row 46 has been completed. 95 sts.

### Raglan Shaping

Cont from chart, dec 1 st at each end of row 47 and every foll alt row until row 76 has been completed. 65 sts.

**77th row** K 2 tog M, k 12 M, 1 C, 6 M, 6 B, 1 D, 2 A, sl 1, k 1 A, psso, k 1 A, k 2 tog A, 2 A, 1 D, 7 B, 18 M, k 2 tog tbl M. Ignoring shaded areas which represent decreased sts, cont from chart, working 1 dec either side of centre st on every 4th row, AND AT THE SAME TIME, dec at each end of every right-side row until row 88 has been completed. 47 sts.

Cont to dec at centre as before, AND AT THE SAME TIME, dec at each end of every row until row 100 has been completed.

Leave rem 17 sts on a stitch holder.

## NECKBAND

Join raglan seams.

With right side facing, using 6½ mm

needles and M, k 5 sts from right front safety pin, pick up and k 5 sts up right front neck, k 17 sts of right sleeve, 23 sts of back neck and 17 sts of left sleeve, pick up and k 5 sts down left front neck then k across 5 sts on left front safety pin. 77 sts.

**Dec row** P 10, *p 2 tog, p 3; rep from * 10 times, p 2 tog, p 10. 65 sts. Work the 8 rows of Chart 1 as for back, working the 8 patt sts 8 times. Change to 5½ mm needles and M. K 1 row. K 1 row to mark hemline. Beg K, st-st 9 rows. Cast off.

## LEFT FRONT BAND

With right side facing, using 6½ mm needles and M, pick up and k 97 sts evenly between neckband hemline and lower hemline.

Beg p, and working from left to right on row 1, work 8 rows of Chart 1 as for back, working the 8 patt sts 12 times.

Change to 5½ mm needles and M. P 1 row. P 1 row to mark hemline. Beg p, st-st 8 rows. Cast off loosely. To neaten upper and lower edges – with right side facing, using 6½ mm needles and M, pick up and k 7 sts along patt section only. Cast off knitwise.

Work right front band to match.

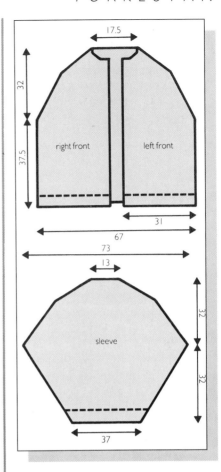

## SHOULDER PAD COVERS

**Make 2** With 5½ mm needles and M, cast on 69 sts.

Decreasing 1 st at each end of 3rd row and on the foll alt row, work 4 rows in k 1, p 1 rib, then st-st 2 rows. 65 sts.

**7th row** K 2 tog, k 28, sl 1, k 1, psso, k 1, k 2 tog, k 28, k 2 tog tbl.

**8th row** P.

The last 2 rows correspond to rows 77 and 78 of Chart 5.

Cont to shape as chart until 17 sts rem, but omitting colour changes. Cast off.

## MAKING UP

Press carefully. Turn down neckband hem and catch down. Join side and sleeve seams. Turn up lower hem and catch down. Turn in hems of front bands and catch down along cast-off edge, then back stitch at neck and lower edges. Turn in sleeve hems and catch down. On wrong side place shoulder pad covers at top of sleeves with p sides tog and sew along raglan seams and at neckband edge. Leave rib edge open to insert detachable shoulder pads.

E·C·L·I·P·S·E

# WHITE HOT

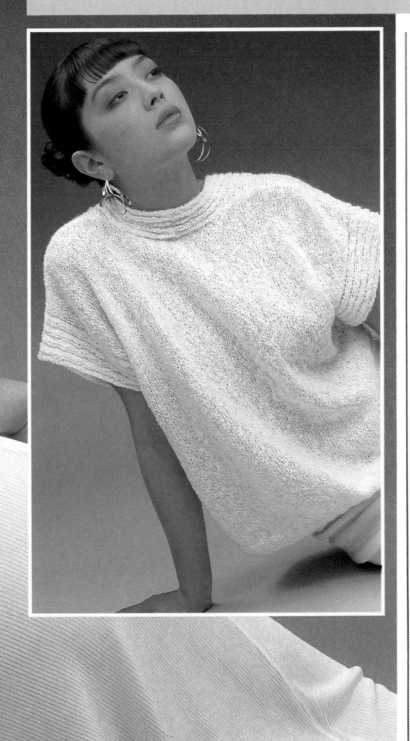

## *ECLIPSE*

*U*NDERSTATED SIMPLICITY IN FRONT CHANGES DRAMATICALLY AT THE BACK, WHERE CONTINUOUS RIB EDGINGS ARE LINKED TO HOLD THE TWO SIDES TOGETHER – AN ELEGANT WAY TO MAKE AN EXIT. DESIGNED BY PHYLLIS SANBAR

### MATERIALS
5 (5, 6) × 50 g balls Sirdar Sombrero
Pair 3¼ mm (No 10) knitting needles
2 spare needles
2 stitch holders

### MEASUREMENTS
To fit bust 86 (91, 97) cm, 34 (36, 38) in
Actual measurement – 98 (107, 115) cm, 38½ (42, 45) in
Length – 58 cm
Figures in brackets are for larger sizes

### TENSION
24 sts and 32 rows to 10 cm over st-st on 3¼ mm needles

### ABBREVIATIONS
alt – alternate; beg – beginning; cm – centimetres; cont – continue; dec – decrease; foll – following; in – inches; inc – increase; k – knit; p – purl; rem – remaining; rep – repeat; sl – slip; st(s) – stitch(es); st-st – stocking stitch

### FRONT
With 3¼ mm needles, cast on 90 (98, 106) sts.

**1st rib row (right side)** K 2, *p 2, k 2; rep from * to end.

**2nd rib row** P 2, *k 2, p 2; rep from * to end.

Rep last 2 rows 6 times, then work 1st rib row again.

**Inc row** Rib 0 (2, 3), *inc in next st, rib 2; rep from * to last 0 (0, 1) st, rib 0 (0, 1). 120 (130, 140) sts.

Beg with a k row, work 90 rows in st-st.

## Armband Shaping

**1st row** Cast on 4 sts, work k 2, p 2 across cast-on sts, k to end.

**2nd row** Cast on 4 sts, work p 2, k 2 across cast-on sts, p to last 4 sts, p 2, k 2.

**3rd row** Cast on 4 sts, work k 2, p 2 across cast-on sts, work as set to end.

**4th row** Cast on 4 sts, work p 2, k 2 across cast-on sts, work as set to end.

Rep 3rd and 4th rows 3 times, thus a total of 20 sts have been cast on at each end and these are worked in rib. 160 (170, 180) sts.

Keeping 20 sts at each end in rib and rem sts in st-st, work 59 rows.

## Neck Shaping

**1st row (wrong side)** Work 67 (72, 77) sts, cast off next 26 sts, work to end.

Cont on last 67 (72, 77) sts only for 1st side and leave rem sts on a spare needle.

Dec 1 st at neck edge on the next 5 rows, then on the foll 2 alt rows. Work 1 row straight.

Cast off rem 60 (65, 70) sts.

With right side facing, rejoin yarn to inner end of sts on spare needle and complete to match 1st side.

## BACK

With 3¼ mm needles, cast on 50 (54, 58) sts for left back.

Work 1st and 2nd rib rows of front 7 times, then work 1st rib row again.

**Inc row** *Rib 1, inc in next st, rib 1; rep from * 9 (10, 11) times, rib 20 (21, 22). 60 (65, 70) sts.

Cont in st-st with ribbed border thus:

**1st row (right side)** Rib 20, k to end.

**2nd row** P to last 20 sts, rib to end.

Rep 1st and 2nd rows 24 times.

***Next row** Rib 18 turn and leave rem 42 (47, 52) sts on a spare needle.

Rib 8 rows on these 18 sts then sl the 18 sts on to a stitch holder. Do not break off yarn*.

With 3¼ mm needles, cast on 50 (54, 58) sts for right back.

Work 1st and 2nd rib rows of front 7 times, then work 1st rib row again.

**Inc row** Rib 20 (21, 22), *rib 1, inc in next st, rib 1; rep from * to end. 60 (65, 70) sts.

Cont in st-st with ribbed border thus:

**1st row (right side)** K to last 20 sts, rib to end.

**2nd row** Rib 20 sts, P to end.

Rep 1st and 2nd rows 24 times, then work 1st row again.

****Next row** Rib 18 turn and leave rem 42 (47, 52) sts on a spare needle. Rib 8 rows on these 18 sts.

**Joining row** Rib across these 18 sts, then work p 2, k 40 (45, 50) across sts on left back spare needle. 60 (65, 70) sts**.

Work 9 rows as set, then rep from * to *.

**Joining row** With wrong side facing, rib across 18 sts on 1st stitch holder, then working behind 2nd stitch holder work k 2 and p 40 (45, 50) across sts on right back spare needle.

Work 9 rows as set, then rep from ** to ** noting that on joining row, after working rib, work behind sts on stitch holder.

Work 9 rows as set, then rep from * to *.

**Joining row** With wrong side facing and working behind spare needles and last stitch holder, rib across 18 sts on 1st stitch holder then k 2 and p 40 (45, 50) across sts on right back spare needle.

Work 9 rows as set, then rep from ** to ** noting that on joining row work behind sts on stitch holder.

Work 20 rows as set, thus ending at side edge.

## Armband Shaping

**1st row** Cast on 4 sts, work p 2, k 2 across cast-on sts, p to last 20 sts, rib 20.

**2nd row** Rib 20, k to last 4 sts, p 2, k 2.

**3rd row** Cast on 4 sts, work p 2, k 2 across cast-on sts, p 2, k 2, p to last 20 sts, rib 20.

**4th row** Rib 20, k to last 8 sts, p 2, k 2, p 2, k 2.

Cont in this way, casting on 4 sts at beg of every wrong-side row until a total of 20 sts have been cast on and worked in rib. 80 (85, 90) sts.

Work 71 rows as set, thus ending at armband edge.

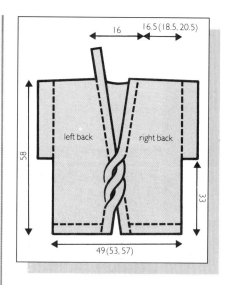

16 · 16.5 (18.5, 20.5)

58

left back · right back

33

49 (53, 57)

## Shoulder Shaping

Cast off 60 (65, 70) sts, rib to end.

Rib 50 rows on rem 20 sts.

Cast off in rib.

With wrong side facing and working behind left back, return to 18 sts on stitch holder, rib 18, then work k 2, p 40 (45, 50) across sts of right back.

Work 18 rows as set, thus ending at side edge.

## Armband Shaping

**1st row** Cast on 4 sts, work k 2, p 2 across cast-on sts, k to last 20 sts, rib 20.

**2nd row** Rib 20, p to last 4 sts, k 2, p 2.

**3rd row** Cast on 4 sts, work k 2, p 2 across cast-on sts, k 2, p 2, k to last 20 sts, rib 20.

**4th row** Rib 20, p to last 8 sts, k 2, p 2, k 2, p 2.

Cont in this way, casting on 4 sts at beg of every right-side row until a total of 20 sts have been cast on and worked in rib. 80 (85, 90) sts.

Work 71 rows as set, thus ending at armband edge.

## Shoulder Shaping

Cast off all 80 (85, 90) sts.

## MAKING UP

Join left shoulder seam. Join right shoulder seam extending seam across cast-off sts of ribbed borders. Sew free row-ends of ribbed border around front neck. Join side and armband seams. Press seams lightly.

# MERIDIAN

A SOFT RIBBED TUBE WITH A SINGLE INTERTWINING CABLE AND A CLOSE-FITTING POLO NECK IS AN ESSENTIAL PART OF A SUMMER WARDROBE. DESIGNED BY CAROLINE INGRAM

## MATERIALS
8 (8, 9) × 50 g balls Jarol Cotton 2000 Double Knitting
Pair each 2¾ mm (No 12), 3 mm (No 11) and 3¾ mm (No 9) knitting needles
Cable needle

## MEASUREMENTS
To fit bust 81 (86, 91) cm, 32 (34, 36) in
Actual measurement – 78 (86, 91) cm, 31 (34, 36) in, slightly stretched
Length – 60 cm
Figures in brackets are for larger sizes

## TENSION
26 sts and 30 rows to 10 cm measured over slightly stretched rib on 3¾ mm needles

## ABBREVIATIONS
beg – beginning; c 6 b – sl next 3 sts on to cable needle and hold at back, k 3 then k 3 from cable needle; c 6 f – sl next 3 sts on to cable needle and hold at front, k 3 then k 3 from cable needle; c 12 b – sl next 6 sts on to cable needle and hold at back, k 6 then k 6 from cable needle; c 12 f – sl next 6 sts on to cable needle and hold at front, k 6 then k 6 from cable needle; cm – centimetres; cont – continue; dec – decrease; in – inches; inc – increase; k – knit; m 1 – make 1 st by picking up the strand between sts and k it through the back of the loop; p – purl; patt – pattern; rem – remain(ing); rep – repeat; sl – slip; st(s) – stitch(es); tog – together.
Work instructions in square brackets the number of times given

## BACK
With 2¾ mm needles, cast on 102 (110, 118) sts.
**1st rib row (right side)** P 2, *k 2, p 2; rep from * to end.
**2nd rib row** K 2, *p 2, k 2; rep from * to end.
Rep 1st and 2nd rib rows for 5 cm, ending with a 1st rib row.
**Inc row** Rib 49 (53, 57), m 1, rib 4, m 1, rib 49 (53, 57). 104 (112, 120) sts.
Change to 3¾ mm needles.
Cont in patt thus:
**1st row (right side)** K 4 (0, 4), [p 2, k 6] 5 (6, 6) times, p 2, k 6, p 1, k 5, p 2, [k 6, p 2] 5 (6, 6) times, k 4 (0, 4).

**2nd row** P 4 (0, 4), [k 2, p 6] 5 (6, 6) times, k 2, p 5, k 1, p 6, k 2, [p 6, k 2] 5 (6, 6) times, p 4 (0, 4).
**3rd row** K 4 (0, 4), [p 2, k 6] 5 (6, 6) times, p 2, c 6 f, p 1, k 5, p 2, [k 6, p 2] 5 (6, 6) times, k 4 (0, 4).
**4th row** As 2nd row.
**5th to 8th rows** As 1st to 4th rows.
**9th and 10th rows** As 1st and 2nd rows.
**11th row** K 4 (0, 4), [p 2, k 6] 5 (6, 6) times, p 2, c 12 b, p 2, [k 6, p 2] 5 (6, 6) times, k 4 (0, 4).
**12th row** P 4 (0, 4), [k 2, p 6] 5 (6, 6) times, k 2, p 6, k 1, p 5, k 2, [p 6, k 2] 5 (6, 6) times, p 4 (0, 4).

**13th row** K 4 (0, 4), [p 2, k 6] 5 (6, 6) times, p 2, k 5, p 1, k 6, p 2, [k 6, p 2] 5 (6, 6) times, k 4 (0, 4).

**14th row** As 12th row.

**15th row** K 4 (0, 4), [p 2, k 6] 5 (6, 6) times, p 2, k 5, p 1, c 6 b, p 2, [k 6, p 2] 5 (6, 6) times, k 4 (0, 4).

**16th row** As 12th row.

**17th to 28th rows** Rep 13th to 16th rows 3 times.

**29th and 30th rows** As 13th and 14th rows.

**31st row** K 4 (0, 4), [p 2, k 6] 5 (6, 6) times, p 2, c 12 f, p 2, [k 6, p 2] 5 (6, 6) times, k 4 (0, 4).

**32nd row** As 2nd row.

**33rd to 40th rows** Rep 1st to 4th rows twice.

These 40 rows form patt.

Patt straight until back measures 36 cm, ending with a wrong-side row.

### Armhole Shaping

Keeping patt correct, cast off 5 (6, 7) sts at beg of next 2 rows.

Dec 1 st at each end of every row until 74 (76, 78) sts rem.**

Patt straight until work measures 57 cm, ending with a wrong-side row.

### Neck Shaping

**1st row** Patt 25 (26, 27) sts, turn.

Cont on these sts only, leaving rem sts on spare needle.

Dec 1 st at neck edge on next 10 rows. 15 (16, 17) sts.

Cast off loosely.

**Next row** With right side facing, sl centre 24 sts on to a stitch holder, rejoin yarn to inner edge of rem 25 (26, 27) sts and patt to end. Complete

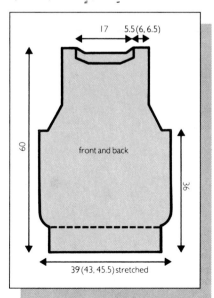

17   5.5 (6, 6.5)

60

front and back

36

39 (43, 45.5) stretched

to match 1st side.

### FRONT

Work as back to **.

Patt straight until front measures 53 cm, ending with a wrong-side row.

### Neck Shaping

**1st row** Patt 29 (30, 31) sts, turn.

Cont on these sts only, leaving rem sts on a spare needle.

Dec 1 st at neck edge on next 14 rows. 15 (16, 17) sts.

Patt straight until front matches back to shoulder.

Cast off loosely.

**Next row** With right side facing, sl centre 16 sts on to a stitch holder, rejoin yarn to inner edge of rem 29 (30, 31) sts and patt to end.

Complete to match 1st side.

### COLLAR

Join right shoulder seam.

With right side facing, using 2¾ mm needles, pick up and k 28 sts evenly down left front neck, patt across 16 sts at centre front thus: p 2, k 2, p 2, k 1, k 2 tog, p 2, k 2 tog, k 1, p 2; pick up and k 28 sts up right front neck, pick up and k 14 sts down right back neck, patt across 24 sts at centre back thus: [p 2, k 2] twice, p 2, k 1, k 2 tog, p 2, k 2 tog, k 1, p 2, k 2, p 2; pick up and k 14 sts up left back neck. 120 sts.

Work 10 cm in p 2, k 2 rib.

Change to 3 mm needles.

Cont straight until rib measures 19 cm.

Cast off loosely in rib.

### ARMBANDS

Join left shoulder and collar seam, reversing collar seam for last 14 cm to allow for turn-over.

With right side facing and using 3 mm needles, pick up and k 150 (154, 158) sts evenly around armhole.

Work 5 rows k 2, p 2 rib as given for back.

Cast off in rib.

### MAKING UP

Join side and armband seams. Press seams only.

# BACK TO BASICS

## SIZING

As you can't try on a design before you start to knit and you don't have a paper pattern for guidance, do look critically at the measurements and proportions of what you intend to make. The fit of these designs varies so much – from a singlet that is under-sized and intended to cling to several deliberately over-sized sweaters – that actual measurements of the finished garments have been given throughout. Look at all the figures given and, if you're in doubt, make a comparison by measuring clothes you already have.

## TENSION

Of course, if your garment is to be the size specified it must be knitted to the correct tension. The idea of knitting a sample square before starting on the whole seems awfully tedious but it is essential for accuracy. It is equally important to measure the finished square scrupulously. Too many knitters (and designers) measure the tension that they want to see. The best way is to count the rows and stitches stated in the tension guide and mark these with pins. Then measure between the markers and see if you have the correct length. If you are over the given measurement use a smaller needle size, if you are under use a larger needle size. Remember that the stated needle size is only a recommendation.

## SHOULDER PADS

Many of these designs are intended to take shoulder pads, so the width of shoulder and depth of armhole have been calculated accordingly. Where the shoulder is a neat, squared-off shape a conventional pair of pads is appropriate. But some of the really large shoulders, especially the raglans, are designed to take the new moulded shapes with adhesive strip which are sold in most department stores and specialist shops. It's very convenient to detach them for storage. Big shoulders also have the advantage of making the waist and hips look smaller by comparison.

## CHARTS

These are used to give the pattern in most types of colour knitting. Occasionally they are also used to convey stitch patterns. If you haven't used them before don't be put off. Once you have mastered the key you will find you have a very clear visual explanation of the stitch.

## COLOUR KNITTING

In Fair Isle technique with colour patterns repeating along a row, the colour not in use is stranded across the back of the work. Always strand the colours in the same sequence and don't pull the strand too tight. Spreading out the last few stitches on the right hand needle before stranding will help. If the yarn not in use has to be carried over groups of more than six or seven stitches it's usually advisable to weave it in at intervals. To weave in, take the second colour over the colour in use just before making a stitch. Take care to make a firm stitch and again, don't take the yarn across too tightly.

With large areas of colour it's better to use the motif or intarsia technique. That is, use a separate small ball of yarn for each area of colour. If there are many areas being worked simultaneously it's a good idea to wind a few metres of yarn on to small plastic or cardboard shuttles. Darning in the ends afterwards is preferable to untangling a lot of yarn as you work. At every colour change the two yarns should be twisted to prevent a hole forming. This simply means crossing one yarn over the other between stitches to lock the two areas together.

Swiss Darning is embroidery over the top of a stitch to change the colour. If the knitted stitch is seen as a V, the needle is taken through the point of the V from the back, then under the two strands of the stitch above from right to left, then back into the point of the V from front to back. This stitch should duplicate the knitted stitch exactly.

## MAKING UP

The iron symbol on the ball band indicates if the yarn can be pressed and at what temperature. Do read the ball band carefully. As a general rule, natural fibres can be damp-pressed but synthetic fibres are better dry-pressed or not pressed at all. To damp-press your work, pin out the pieces, right side down. Using the measurement diagrams as a guide, square the pieces up so that rows and stitches run at perfect right angles. Press, using a thin, damp cloth under a warm iron. It's impossible to revive over-pressed work but under-pressing is not making the most of your knitting. Don't press ribs at all and be careful not to flatten textured stitches. Press seams as you sew them up.

## AFTERCARE

Keep a ball band and refer to it for washing and dry cleaning instructions. It's better not to use harsh detergents even if a yarn is machine washable. A cool or cold water wash is suitable for most hand knitting. Don't wring out, just squeeze gently and dry flat or spin dry in a pillow case. Never hang knitting up, especially when it's made heavier by being wet. When the garment is damp it should be eased into shape.

Knitting is a very elastic fabric and its shape and texture can be drastically altered by washing and pressing. Do make sure that you improve yours!

# LIST OF SUPPLIERS

In case of difficulty obtaining any of the products mentioned please contact the company concerned. If you write, please enclose a stamped addressed envelope. Mail order details can usual,y be supplied in addition to information about stockists.

**ANNY BLATT**
Anny Blatt UK Ltd
Ambergate
Derby DE5 2EY
Tel: 077 385 6025

**ARGYLL**
Argyll Wools Ltd
PO Box 15
Priestley Mills
Pudsey
West Yorkshsire LS28 9LT
Tel: 0532 558411

**AVOCET**
Hammond Associates Ltd
Hammerain House
Hookstone Avenue
Harrogate
North Yorkshire HG2 8ER
Tel: 0423 871481

**COPLEY**
L Copley Smith & Sons
PO Box 46
Darlington
Co Durham DL1 1YW
Tel: 0325 460133

**ELLS & FARRIER LTD**
5 Princes, Street
London W1R 8PH
Tel: 629 9964

Mail Order:
Unit 26
Chiltern Trading Estate
Holmer Green
High Wycombe
Buckinghamshire
Tel: 0494 715606

**EMU**
Emu. Wools Ltd
Leeds Road
Greengate
Bradford
West Yorkshire BD10 9TE
Tel: 0274 614031

**GEORGES PICAUD**
Priory Yarns Ltd
24 Prospect Road
Ossett
West Yorkshire WF5 8AE
Tel: 0924 262138

**HAYFIELD**
Hayfield Textiles Ltd
Glusburn
Keighley
West Yorkshire BD20 8QP
Tel: 0535 33333

**JAEGER**
Jaeger Hand Knitting Ltd
Alloa
Clackmannanshire
Scotland FK10 2EG
Tel: 0259 723431

**JAROL**
White Rose Mills
Cape Street
Canal Road
Bradford BD1 4RN
Tel: 0274 392274

**KING COLE**
R J Cole Ltd
Merrie Mills
Old Souls Way
Bingley BD16 2AX
Tel: 0274 561331

**LISTER**
Lister Handknitting
PO Box 37
Whiteoak Mills
Wakefield
West Yorkshire WF2 9SF
Tel: 0924 375311

**MAXWELL CARTLIDGE**
(Mail order only)
PO Box 33
Colchester
Essex
Tel: 07875 2111

**PATONS**
Patons & Baldwins Ltd
Alloa
Clackmannanshire
Scotland FK10 2EG
Tel: 0259 723431

**PHILDAR**
4 Gambrel Road
Westgate Industrial Estate
Northampton NN5 5NF
Tel: 0604 583111

**PINGOUIN**
7-11 Lexington Street
London W1R 4BU
Tel: 439 8891

**POPPLETON**
Richard Poppleton & Sons
Albert Mills
Horbury
Wakefield
West Yorkshire WF4 5NJ
Tel: 0924 264141

**ROBIN**
Robin Wools Ltd
Robin Mills
Idle
Bradford
West Yorkshire BD10 9TE
Tel: 0274 612561

**ROWAN**
Green Lane Mill
Washpit
Holmfirth
Huddersfield
West Yorkshire HD7 1RN
Tel: 0484 686714

**SAMBAND**
Viking Wools Ltd
Rothay Holme
Rothay Road
Ambleside
Cumbria LA22 0HQ
Tel: 0966 32991

**SCHACHENMAYR**
Box No 2
Edward Street
Redditch
Worcestershire B97 6HB
Tel: 0527 67771

**SCHEEPJESWOL**
PO Box 48
7 Colemeadow Road
North Moons Moat
Redditch
Worcestershire B98 9NZ
Tel: 0527 61056

**SIRDAR**
Sidar PLC
Consumer Service Department
Flanshaw Lane
Alverthorpe
Wakefield
West Yorkshire WF2 9ND
Tel: 0924 371501

**3 SUISSES**
Marlborough House
38 Welford Road
Leicester LE2 7AA
Tel: 0533 554713

**SUNBEAM**
Sunbeam Knitting Wools
Crawshaw Mills
Pudsey
West Yorkshire LS28 7BS
Tel: 0532 571871

**TOOTAL KNIT YARNS**
Tootal Craft Ltd
56 Oxford Street
Manchester M60 1HJ
Tel: 061 228 0474

**TWILLEYS**
H G Twilley Ltd
Roman Mill
Stamford
Lincolnshire PE9 1BG
Tel: 0780 52661

**WENDY**
Carter & Parker Ltd
Gordon Mills
Netherfield Road
Guisely
Leeds
West Yorkshire LS20 9PD
Tel: 0943 72264

**YARNWORKS**
4th Floor
Waring & Gillow Building
Western Avenue
London W3 0TA
Tel: 01 993 6061

# ACKNOWLEDGMENTS

A guide to the clothes and accessories featured:

**ROSE QUARTZ** (page 8)
suit and earrings: Fenwick, New Bond Street, London W1; belt: Hobbs, South Molton Street, London W1; bracelet: Detail, Endell Street, London WC2

**AMETHYST** (page 11)
suit: Whistles, St Christopher's Place, London W1; jewellery: Michaela Frey, South Molton Street, London W1; gloves: Dents from Attitudes at Moss Bros

**BON CHIC** (page 14)
necklaces and bracelets: John Lewis, London W1; earrings: Pink Soda at Miss Selfridge; skirt and polo neck jumper: Fenwick; velvet gloves: Dents; shoes: Hobbs; beret: The Hat Shop, Neal Street, London WC2

**SYCAMORE** (page 18)
breeches: Laurence Corner, Hampstead Road, London NW1; hat: Blax, Sicilian Avenue, London WC2; lace blouse: Capricorn, Kensington Park Road, London W11; brooch: John Wind at Harvey Nichols; stick: Fulton; gloves: Dents

**SILVER BIRCH** (page 22)
breeches: Laurence Corner; earrings: Blax; stick: Fulton; string-back gloves: Dents; hat: model's own

**NORTHERN LIGHTS** (page 26)
leggings: Fitness Centre, Langley Street, London WC2; gloves: Fenwick

**FINE ROMANCE** (page 30)
earrings: Detail; bracelet: Blax; fabrics: John Lewis

**KNIGHTSBRIDGE** (page 34)
beret, polo neck jumper and tights: Fenwick; brooch: Detail; gloves: Dents; shoes: Hobbs

**KENSINGTON** (page 38)
beret and tights: Fenwick; earrings: Detail

**BELGRAVIA** (page 41)
scarf and tights: Fenwick; bracelets: Detail

**SUPERSAMPLER** (page 43)
leggings: Hilary Bockham at Zone, Harvey Nichols; sunglasses and gloves: Fenwick; shoes: Robot; mittens: model's own

**CRIMSON** (page 48)
silk skirt: Linda Powell, 62 Triton Road, London SE21; bracelet: Michaela Frey; earrings: Van Peterson, Walton Street, London SW3

**SCARLET** (page 51)
dress: Benetton; jet bracelets: Michaela Frey; earrings: Van Peterson

**VERMILION** (page 55)
dress: Whistles; earrings: Van Peterson

**PERFECT PARTNERS** (page 58)
skirt: Whistles; jewellery: Michaela Frey; brocade hat: The Hat Shop

**DELHI** (page 62)
skirt: Jeffrey Rogers; bracelets: John Lewis; hat: The Hat Shop

**MADRAS** (page 66)
lace skirt: Linda Powell; jewellery: Van Peterson

**JAIPUR** (page 69)
leggings: Jeffrey Rogers; hat: Warehouse

**FIFTIES FOREVER** (page 71)
watch: Detail; bracelets: Extras at Hyper Hyper; belt: Fenwick; vest and jeans: model's own

**MARLBOROUGH** (page 74)
trousers, shirt, tie and braces: Blax; brooch worn as tie pin: Fenwick

**WINCHESTER** (page 78)
trousers: Fenwick; socks: Blax; mittens: Laurence Corner; shoes: Hobbs; hat, scarf, raincoat: model's own

**ETON** (page 81)
shorts: Laurence corner; polo neck sweater: Paul Smith, Floral Street, London WC2; watch: Fenwick; tights: Aristoc; spectacles: model's own

**HARROW** (page 84)
belt: Mulberry, Gees Court, London W1; scarf: The Scotch House, Knightsbridge, London SW3; trousers, earrings: model's own

**DENIM DAYS** (page 87)
jeans: Falmers; shirt: C17, James Street, London W1; beret: Laura Ashley; gloves: Laurence Corner; bag and scarf: models own

**BOKHARA** (page 90)
shirt: Benetton; shawl: The Scotch House; jewellery: Catalyst at Hyper Hyper; bowler hat: The Hat Shop; tights: Mary quant; boots: Robot

**TASHKENT** (page 96)
skirt: Benetton; underskirt: Fenwick; blouse: Consumer Guide at Jones, Kings Road, London SW3; shawl: Capricorn; jewellery: Catalyst; gloves: Dents; boots: Robot; tights: Mary Quant; hat: The Hat Shop

**ECLIPSE** (page 102)
skirt: Benetton; earrings: Detail; bracelet: John Lewis

**MERIDIAN** (page 105)
skirt: Benetton; bracelets and earrings: Detail; hat: The Hat Shop

## A·C·K·N·O·W·L·E·D·G·M·E·N·T·S

The book was designed by Polly Dawes

Photography by
Tony Boase: 18, 21, 22, 23, 43, 46, 47, 74, 75, 76, 78, 80, 81, 82, 84, 87, 88
Jill Green and Neil Phillips of Pinsharp: front cover, 8, 10, 11, 13, 30, 31, 58, 59, 61, 90, 91, 96, 97, 101
Heinz Lautenbacher: 48, 49, 50, 51, 54, 55, 56, 62, 63, 64, 66, 67, 68, 69, 102, 103, 105, 106
Francesca Sullivan: 14, 15, 16, 26, 27, 29, 34, 35, 36, 38, 39, 41, 42, 71, 72

Photographic styling by Marie Willey
Make-up by Kim Jacob of Pin-Up
Hair styled by Jaffa of Pin-Up

Instructions written and styled by Sue Horan
Instructions checked by Marilyn Wilson
Charts and diagrams by Jeremy Firth